The French Family Of East Anglia's Story

A STUDY OF THE RISE AND RISE OF THE MIDDLE CLASSES

JUDITH S CAMPBELL

SERENDIPITY

First published in 2003 by
Serendipity
Suite 530
37 Store Street
Bloomsbury
London

British Library Cataloguing-in-Publication data
A record for this book is available from the British Library

ISBN 1 84394 068 x

Printed and bound in Europe by the Alden Group, Oxford

Contents

*To my beloved husband Ian who
always encouraged my research and said
I should write such a book*

Acknowledgements

To Jonathan and Tass for all their help
and support with the project and for
Paul who made me do it and has also
given me a great deal of help and
encouragement.

To all the Record Offices I have used
especially the Public Record Office at
Kew as well as those in Suffolk and
Essex who have assisted me in my
research so well and enabled the book to
be written.

CHAPTER I

Introduction

From today's perspective when nearly everyone considers himself or herself to be middle class, a number of the concepts of the rise of the middle classes are bizarre indeed. However this situation has only arisen after the Second World War and started with Attlee's Landslide Labour Government victory of 1945. This success had been brought about, in the main, by the votes of the middle class young men and women who had fought alongside their working class contemporaries in the war.

In 1942, Sir William Beveridge had issued his famous report on Social Insurance and Allied Services. This was a revolutionary scheme to give financial support to the unemployed, the sick and the elderly. Beveridge's idea was to end all freedom from want and more importantly to abolish the much hated Victorian Poor Law of means testing, which had itself evolved from the Speenhamland System of Elizabeth the First. He therefore made his recommendations for a flat rate system of unemployment, sickness and old age benefits. However Beveridge himself hated the concept of the Welfare State and always insisted that his aim was not to take away any personal responsibility.

The Labour Government implemented Beveridge's reforms in the Health and Social Security systems almost immediately after they were returned to Parliament. They established a free Health Service for all and also gave everyone a right to a pension, which was introduced in full together with unemployment payments. At the same time, the 1948 Education Bill was passed which enabled all children to have a good education from the age of five until the age of sixteen at State Junior Schools and subsequently at Grammar, Secondary Modern or Technical schools.

All of these measures together with the increasing wealth of the following Macmillan years of the fifties, when we 'never had it so good,' did a great deal to blur the old class divisions, until today we are all as one, or nearly so.

Throughout history, there has always been a constant movement between the social classes, which can be seen in the endless movement in social space that characterizes a great deal of our history. This is exemplified by some individuals struggling to rise to the class above and others trying equally as hard to maintain their current positions.

During the eighteenth and nineteenth centuries many people believed that the nation's brains, leadership and organizational abilities were in the main derived from the middle classes.

However this term middle class is almost impossible to define and one important question to be addressed is why the term middle classes and not the middle class is so often used. Perhaps we need look no further than William Cobbett who was one of the first to use this plural term. This was further amplified in the book by Brougham, written in 1831, who reflected, that the spirit of the time 'were the middle classes, the wealth and intelligence of the country, the glory of the British name.'

The main attributes of the middle classes cannot be defined purely in financial terms nor even by professional skills. One can find examples of much richer working class men than their middle class counterparts and also in the fact that one teacher considered himself to be middle class and another working class. However as the centuries progressed this group was not only affected by their heredity and environment as everyone was but also they were influenced by the new attitudes, beliefs, education and even the clothes of the changing times. During the period of this study one of the main catalysts of the middle classes can be seen to be the family. Research shows that if a son was in danger of failing financially or in any other way his family would assist. Further the ambitious son often married and founded his own family and by the dint of his efforts moved relentlessly upwards.

During the late seventeenth and early eighteenth centuries, the only means of rising through the class structure had been by marriage. At this time many aristocratic families were falling on hard times and therefore were forced to allow their younger daughters to marry the sons of a lower class if the family was sufficiently rich to make this a worthwhile option. Being a member of the professions also did not ensure being middle class for although a physician was regarded as such, a surgeon was definitely not until over a hundred and fifty years later.

By 1750, the land-owning aristocracy were about to face their biggest challenge in the history of this country. With the advent of the Agricultural Revolution and the Enclosure Acts combined with the Industrial Revolution, many agricultural labourers were dispossessed of their land and the landowners themselves also faced an uncertain future. Many of the more intelligent and resourceful of this group of agricultural workers moved away from the land into the cities where they could work in the newly formed factories. Many of these men subsequently became the new breed of masters. Others also moved out of the old industries and established new ones thereby increasing their own wealth and establishing the base for their rise up the social scale. Further they understood that increasing the means of production on which both they and the country depended had the knock-on result of averting both famine and revolution. Also others began to enter the professions like banking, accountancy and even the veterinary service.

In all these endeavours the main prize was success, with more money and property. Failure however was a grave disaster and meant joining the ever-increasing ranks of the poor. The pinnacle of this rise of the middle classes was the 1851 Great Exhibition at the Crystal Palace, which was organized in the main by Prince Albert and opened by Queen Victoria. This was in fact one of the greatest monuments to their success and endeavour that the county had ever seen.

From 1800 through to 1850 the middle classes also made a great impact on the political scene of the day. They began to take political reform very seriously and were in many ways instrumental in the passing of the Great Reform Bill of 1832, the Factory Acts and the Repeal of the Corn Laws. The latter led to cheap food and increased trade.

Further the novels of people like Charles Dickens and Charles Kingsley had stirred their consciences. This combined with the fact that many of this group of men were also very religious meant that there was a great increase in church building as well as the establishment of the Ragged Schools.

Many years ago I was given some very old birth and marriage certificates by my maternal grandmother which for a long while were left in a safe place to gather dust.

However twelve years ago as I had some spare time my interest was rekindled and so the exploration of my family began.

This piece is part of my researches and concerns my father's family, The French Family. All my father knew of them were his immediate family and grandparents, with all the rest being shrouded in mystery. Over the subsequent years 'the Family' has emerged from the mists of time to interest and intrigue me.

This is their story and that of their continual rise as members of the Middle Classes. It also tells of their trials and tribulations as well as their triumphs and good times.

CHAPTER 2

Harold Gainsford French 1914–2000

Harold lived his life against a backdrop of great changes. He was born a month before the Great War and also was a young married man during the Second World War. This was a period of countless revolutions abroad together with the rise and fall of Dictators. At the same time there was the Great World-wide Depression, which hit both rich and poor alike. During this period, England was more of a democracy than its European neighbours. It was developing its own Welfare State as well as the foundations of what would eventually make it the centre of a multi-racial Commonwealth. Further it was a period of unprecedented technical change with the development of the aeroplane, space flights, travel and the general increase in electrical machinery to make industry and the home the place it is today.

My father Harold Gainsford was born on 14 July 1914 in Wanstead. He was the third child of William and Evelyn French who lived at 60 Chester Road. This was a fine old Victorian house with three bedrooms and a large lounge and dining room. It also had an elaborate wrought iron balcony at the front and a good sized garden at the back in which the three children could play. Maisie was the eldest and she had been born on 9 April 1911 and her brother Wilfred was born in November 1912.

Harold was baptized at Trinity Presbyterian Church at

Maryland Point Stratford where his parents had been married. This was his mother's church and that of all her family.

The three children had a very happy childhood with plenty of opportunities to enjoy nature, and for my father especially, the bird life. He went to a private school Gowan Lea in Wanstead where he stayed until 1926.

Although this was the year of the General Strike, it was also a momentous year for the French family. My grandfather had decided to move out of Wanstead and live in the peaceful village of Loughton.

Loughton is situated on the edge of Epping Forest, which he and the family had grown to love so much when they lived in Wanstead as they had spent many hours walking there. Historically Loughton had always been very proud of the Village Hamden, as Loughton was originally called. Loughton had been saved together with Epping Forest from being stolen from its people and their most famous citizen was Thomas Willingale and he it was who had fought for the freedom of the forestland to remain as common land. Thomas was a very poor man who made his living by gathering wood and grazing his animals in the forest. In the mid 1850s the common lands of England were being enclosed and sold and it soon became apparent that the Crown's rights to Epping Forest were also going to be sold, and thus the Loughton villagers would lose their common law rights to grazing. Even though Willingale was a very old man, he led the fight for the preservation of the beauty spot which was Epping Forest. After 15 years of both Parliamentary and Court battles, the people of Loughton gained the support of the Corporation of London and finally a Royal Commission found that Willingale was right and that the enclosure of the forest was illegal in this instance. The Corporation of London then spent a great deal of money on the forest and finally Epping Forest was declared free for the people. Queen Victoria came down to Chingford and opened the area of 6,800 acres, which was to remain a public place for grazing and for the enjoyment of the people forever. Willingale's fight was commemorated forever by the forest itself.

When William French and his family arrived in Loughton it was connected to the City by steam train, which made it easy for William to get to his own firm for work. It was also near to Epping Forest.

William found a wonderful site to build a home, which was near the top of Alderton Hill with good views all around. He then set about designing his new house and garden himself. The result was a house with a huge lounge and a loggia overlooking the tennis court in the garden. There was also a dining room, which accommodated a billiard table as well as being used for meals. In the front of the house was a big study and kitchen as well as a walk-in pantry, which was most important in the twenties, with marble shelves to maximize the cold there. A scullery where the cooker and sink were situated was off the kitchen. Upstairs there were four large bedrooms and a bathroom and a boxroom as well as a separate WC, which was a great innovation.

William then turned his attention to the garden area. Outside the back of the house, he planted a ceonothus to cover the walls and also two rose beds. A grass slope went down to the tennis court, which was surrounded by gardens, filled with flowering shrubs and perennial borders. My father gave them a lovely flowering cherry tree years later to commemorate my birth.

Near the end of the lefthand side he constructed a well to supplement the water supply and beyond the tennis court was a goldfish pond and a large apple orchard which supplied us all for the whole winter. All fruit was eaten in sequence which meant having to eat a horrid but nevertheless pretty apple, the Quarandon, first. He then placed a croquet lawn beyond the orchard, which was later turned into a chicken run during the war to keep us in eggs.

At the front of the house he put in two laurel bushes and two large conifers and called the house 'The Laurels'.

On moving to Loughton, my father joined his brother at the Forest School. He was a very studious boy much enjoying mathematics and history. Forest School was an Oxford Movement establishment so was very High Church, which Harold found difficult as his formative years had been within the Presbyterian congregation. However he came under the influence of the very devout Headmaster Mr Ralph Guy who took the boys for divinity and also for confirmation classes. On 2 April 1928, Harold was confirmed, with his brother, in the school chapel. It was also during this time that Harold began his great interest in the Bible, and over the years he knew it backwards and forwards, which was good for his three daughters who were taught by him.

Harold was very unlike his brother and sister who were more interested in practical affairs and sport. However they did persuade Harold to play tennis and he became a very good club player at the Avenue Club, which the three joined to be with a wider group of players.

During this happy period, my father together with his father, brother, sister and Bob the dog spent a great deal of time in Epping Forest walking and watching the wildlife, especially the birds. From this youthful experience my father started his lifelong interest and love of birds and all wildlife in the forest. He also knew his way around the many paths deep in the forest and later on in life took us and many church groups on numerous walks and picnics and blackberrying expeditions.

Harold got distinction in his matriculation and was offered a place at Oxford University to read History. Sadly the timing was not right for him as Britain and the rest of the world were struggling under the weight of the Depression. As a result Harold's father decided that it was better for him to get a profession and go to work. Harold decided, therefore, to become a Chartered Accountant, and passed his final examination in May 1936, although it was always a matter of regret not to have gone to university. After his finals, he was articled to the firm of Accountants, Casselton and Elliott in the City of London. Harold received no salary and his father paid for his apprenticeship and supported him until he was 22 years old. During this time he worked like a dogsbody during the day and studied for his examinations at night.

By 1937, he and his brother and sister were very much involved in the tennis life of the Avenue Tennis Club, with Maisie being the Tennis Captain. One particularly hot afternoon in April 1935, she was asked to give a playing test for a new member, Elsie Last. She was the daughter of Minnie Last whose husband William had died when Elsie was only ten years old. William came from an agricultural home in Suffolk in the peninsular just north of my home here at Felixstowe. When he was sixteen years old, he joined the Merchant Navy and was later involved with Lord Grey's ill-fated Tourmaline expedition to North Africa in 1898. Minnie and her family had lived in the shadow of the Tower of London all their lives and it was to her home that William came for lodgings when he came to London, and they were married when Minnie became nineteen.

On the hot afternoon in question, Harold and Wilfred were relaxing in the garden at the Laurels. Maisie eventually persuaded them to make up a foursome. Harold had never been very interested in the opposite sex but that all changed on meeting Elsie that afternoon. After a year-long courtship, they became engaged and Elsie joined the family in April 1937 for their annual Easter holiday to Eastbourne. The couple were married at Barking Abbey Church on 9 April 1938, which was Maisie's birthday.

Elsie wore a beautiful pink flowered lace dress with a matching bonnet trimmed with pink velvet. After the wedding they went on honeymoon to Lynmouth and stayed at The Rising Sun Hotel like Harold's parents before them.

I was born on the 1 January 1941 at the height of the Second World War. We lived at 48 Lower Park Road, which my father had bought when he married in 1938. It was a very pretty little house in Loughton which was very near the village, as Loughton still was then, and also close to the station which enabled my father to get to his work in the City of London at Casselton and Elliot.

At the outbreak of the war, my parents had an Anderson Shelter built in the garden, which became my second home and from where I saw the first doodlebug bomb.

When I was three years old I attended Miss Coleman's School which was round the corner. At the age of four, I started at Oakland's where I stayed until I was eleven. I then moved to the Loughton High School where my aunt Maisie French had been a pupil in the 1920s.

During my first year at the High School, I had become very interested in history, which was greatly fostered by my father who also had a very keen interest in the subject. Also at this period, my grandmother Minnie Last was given some old birth and marriage certificates by her sister which she showed me. She also had a number of photographs, which fascinated me, and there was one of her mother as a young woman who was not dissimilar to me in looks. She also had many tales to tell of her own life as well as many family stories, some of which I found to be true and some not so. But that is another and later tale. From these small beginnings came my abiding interest in our family history which later enabled me to trace the French Family back to the early eighteenth century.

I was joined in November 1944 by my sister Jane and in May 1946 by my sister Celia. Both babies proved to be great new playmates as well as real-life dolls.

Life continued during the war to be a hazardous time and our house was only preserved from the bomb which fell opposite by its being detached. All the windows fell out but we were safe. My father was an Air Raid Warden with his father and was on duty most evenings after work.

When Hitler launched his V bombers against London, my mother took me out to watch. Eventually, in 1945, hostilities ended and I went with my parents to Buckingham Palace to see the King and Queen and Winston Churchill come out onto the balcony to be cheered by the crowds.

After the war, we moved to 20 Tycehurst Hill, which was a four-bedroomed house and easily accommodated the larger family. It was a very pleasant house with spacious rooms but oh so cold in the winter. In 1947, England experienced a terrible winter with the snow arriving in late January and staying for more than fifty days. We were frozen up for a long time and with the subsequent thaw and the bomb damage which the house had sustained, the ceilings came down in Jane's and my bedroom. However with the help of some workmen who were working opposite and the local plumber all was easily put to rights.

Life changed a great deal after the war with the slow end to rationing and the arrival of strange new foods such as exotic fruits like bananas, melons and oranges, all of which I liked. However the new eggs were not a patch on the old dried eggs and the cream was not enjoyed like the synthetic cream to which we had grown accustomed.

I enjoyed my years at Oaklands School with the annual plays, the Greek dancing classes and music lessons. So time passed very happily and culminated in a memorable trip to the Festival of Britain and also watching the Queen on her balcony on Coronation Night with my father, followed by the fireworks in Battersea Park.

At eleven, I went to the High School, which I also enjoyed, especially the academic challenges it brought. The years quickly passed with tennis tournaments and Greek dancing competitions and all the fun of dances and other happy pursuits. Then at eighteen I went to Manchester University to read History, which was really a wonderful time both from the work point of view and from the breadth of experience it gave me. Most importantly it brought me great happiness which I had for so many years with my beloved husband Ian. We met on my first day at the Anglican Fellowship Social and were married soon after I graduated. We had two sons, James and Jonathan.

Both Jane and Celia followed the same educational path as me, going to Oaklands School, the High School and then on to University. They also both excelled at tennis. Jane won Junior Wimbledon Girls' Singles in June 1962 and Celia the Mixed Doubles the following year. Jane then read Economics and Celia Mathematics at Exeter and Manchester Universities respectively. Both girls got married and Jane had three children Andrew, Katharine and Paul. Celia became a teacher and then very quickly went into higher education where she became a lecturer at the North London Polytechnic. She later became the youngest Professor of Maths in England at the Department of Education at London University.

During Harold's time at Casselton and Elliotts, he began his long association with the Diamond Trading Company. At this time, the company was a small concern and Harold audited their accounts each year. These were then sent to Johannesburg. Over the years Harold got to know many of the men who worked in the diamond world. Out of the blue, the Managing Director offered Harold the job of Chief Accountant, very casually over a morning cup of coffee. Harold was two years off his fiftieth birthday and had never been abroad before let alone travelled on a newfangled aeroplane. However he accepted with alacrity and thus became a gamekeeper turned poacher!!

There then followed an exciting new career which took Harold all over the world to places like South Africa, Japan, Israel and of course to Antwerp the home of the cut diamonds, despite his inability to speak a foreign language. With his quiet professional reticence he presided over the accounts department for the next eighteen years. He also became a father figure to all his younger colleagues and was not only a fountain of financial information but also a mine of other information from the Bible and Shakespeare to Egyptology and History, which certainly intrigued his colleagues.

Throughout Harold and Elsie's married life, the main cornerstone was the Church of Saint Mary in Loughton.

They worshipped there faithfully for over sixty years and their lives followed the Church's year from Christmas through to Harvest. Harold audited the Church Accounts for fifty years and only raised his fee from nothing to twice nothing thus causing consternation to the Church Warden! Meanwhile Elsie was a very keen member of the Mother's Union.

As well as travelling with his job, Harold and Elsie then went around the world twice to places like Australia, Mexico, Thailand, Fiji and Canada. Because of the ante trust laws, Harold was not allowed to enter the USA, which appealed to him as he felt it gave him a sense of notoriety.

Both Harold and Elsie continued to play tennis at the Loughton and Connaught tennis clubs. Elsie was very soon selected to play for the County and was awarded her County Colours. Throughout their lives, they took many and varied evening classes, which ranged from Egyptology to Literature and Anthropology. They also had a great interest in the Lifeboat Service and the National Trust. However their abiding interest was in birds and both were active life members of the Royal Society for the Protection of Birds.

They both greatly enjoyed their children and grandchildren, taking the latter to their old haunts of West Runton in Norfolk and Felixstowe in Suffolk for numerous holidays.

Life continued very happily for Harold and Elsie except for the two burglaries they had at their lovely third home at Connaught Hill, which had been bought for their retirement in 1969. This was a beautiful 2-bedroom home and garden overlooking their beloved forest.

In 1981 they decided that a move was necessary and moved to a new flat on the other side of the hill, which was equally near to the forest. This is where they lived very happily for the next twenty years.

They celebrated their Ruby Wedding, their Golden Wedding as well as their Diamond Wedding in style. The first two celebrations were very grand dinner and dances: the first at the Tower Hotel by the River Thames in London and the second at the Brewery in Chiswell Street in the City of London. The Diamond Wedding party was held in Chingford at Chasneys restaurant and was likewise a wonderful party, for which they were famous.

Harold died on 6 February 2000.

CHAPTER 3

William Henry French 1881–1965

William's early life was spent during the last years of Queen Victoria's reign. At this time, England was a very stable country under a Constitutional Monarchy and was benefiting from the changes brought about by the Reform Bills of 1884 and 1885, which had increased the manhood suffrage. However Continental Europe was becoming a serious economic competitor as were the United States of America. During William's young adult years, life in England was constantly changing. On the positive side, pensions were established in 1908 and also a scheme of National Health Insurance. As this had to be paid for, it brought an increase in Death Duties and Income Tax, which affected all the working population, although this distributed wealth more equitably. However after the reign of Victoria and Edward with their leisurely way of life, the seeds of the unrest of the post-war era were being sown. The movement for the Emancipation of Women had started and there was also a great deal of trade union unrest, which showed itself in strikes.

William Henry French was born on 8 November 1881 at 1 Cobden Road, Leytonstone. He was the fourth child of John Henry French and his wife Annie. Annie was the second daughter of Richard Bowden Hall, an India rubber worker and his wife Mary Ann. Richard had died when he was 58 years old and after John and Annie were married, Mary Ann came to live with them. John Henry had an elder brother George and two younger brothers Richard Dixon and Gainsford William and one sister Kate. For all his working life, John worked as a clerk in the City of London.

William had a very happy childhood in Leytonstone and was particularly close to his sisters, especially Kate. His brother John was a very quiet and aloof boy and did not share William's tremendous sense of humour and adventure. When William was at school, he played a trick on the young lady who was a pupil teacher at his school. He had always had a great love of nature so when he found a grass snake in the garden he took it to school and placed it in the teacher's desk. When she opened the desk, she let out a great scream of fear. The class was in total consternation. However William stepped up to the desk and grabbed the snake and took it away. He was the hero of the hour.

Likewise one day when he was watching the carters from the city bringing their produce to Leytonstone on their way to Epping, he noticed that many of them were sound asleep as they slowly made their way east. One fine day, he played a further trick. He waited until a cart had stopped in the market place and then carefully as the carter was asleep quietly turned the horse around. Thus the carter would have gone back to the city and would not get to Epping that day.

William was soon joined by Agnes in 1883, Emily in 1886 and Dorothy on 25 November 1889. They had another brother Gainsford who was born on 28 January 1885 but he died a year later of the flu, which turned into pneumonia. This upset William considerably and made a lasting impression on him for the rest of his life. All the children were given pet names which all ended in 'y'. Thus William was Willy and Dorothy Dolly.

William was not only a joker and naturalist but was also a copious reader and a very talented artist. In later life he filled his home with really professional watercolours and oil paintings as well as numerous pen and ink pictures of Essex buildings. He left school at the age of fourteen as was the custom and was trained as a commercial traveller. During this period he experimented with other career options and used to write reports on football matches for the local and the national press. However he found the fighting on the terraces at Millwall F. C. very worrying.

He also used to attend the debates in London in which such people as George Bernard Shaw and HG Wells took part. This sparked off his lifelong interest in all things both cultural and political.

The family moved from Cobden Road to Cann Hall Road before making their final move to 5 Addison Road in Wanstead, which was to be the family home for sixty years. At this time William met a young man with similar interests to himself. His name was Harry Hancock and he later married William's sister Agnes and they continued to be lifelong friends.

One of their mutual interests was walking and on one such holiday to the Lake District they had a very frightening experience. They were climbing up the Great Gable when a mist came down. This happened so suddenly, they immediately stopped in their tracks. Both had the usual walking stick which men carried at the time, and they continued to walk placing the stick in front of them to ensure they were not near any precipice. Suddenly William could not feel anything in front of him and he called to Harry who was behind him to stop. They had been warned that if they felt they were in this

kind of situation they should sit or lie down until the
mist lifted. Both men lay down as darkness was falling
and went to sleep. Next morning they were wakened by
a fellow walker who enquired why they had gone to sleep
in the middle of a field and not under the nearby hedge!!!
In fact William's stick was merely broken.

In the later years of the reign of Edward VII, William
met and fell in love with Evelyn May Rover of Stratford.
She was the third daughter of Frederick James Rover a
Lloyds underwriter and his wife Clara Susannah who
lived in Earlham Grove in West Ham. Frederick Rover
was the third son of Henry Rover. Henry had come to
seek his fortune here from Hanover in 1847 after his own
land had been devastated by repeated crop failures and
also by revolution. On meeting his future wife Caroline
and wanting to buy a house, he was naturalized. He
became a successful engineer and later ran a coffeehouse.
Frederick's wife Clara was the daughter of William and
Ann Houghton who was a widow. Her husband had been
a moderately successful innkeeper for many years and his
widow carried on the business. When she retired from
this work her new son in law paid for a companion and
allowed her to live in his first home when he bought the
house in Earlham Grove.

When she met William, Evelyn was working at the time
in the offices of the Tate and Lyle Sugar Company. Here
she had become very friendly with three of William's
sisters, Agnes, Emily and Dorothy.

On the afternoon of 18 June 1910, they were married
at Trinity Presbyterian Church at Maryland Point. The
service was fully choral and the minister the Reverend
Donald Ross officiated. The church was beautifully
decorated with flowers and Evelyn's future brother in law
Howard Vernon played the organ.

Evelyn wore an ivory white satin dress with a court train, which was trimmed with darned lace and embroidered with pearls. Her four sisters Florence, Grace, Ivy and Eva who wore apricot Liberty silk dresses and picture hats trimmed with roses, lilac and velvet attended her. The best man was Harry Hancock who was William's best friend. During their bachelor years as well as their ill-fated trip to the Lake District, they had spent many happy holidays walking and cycling around England.

After the marriage ceremony there was a reception at Earlham Grove for more than fifty guests. Later in the afternoon William and Evelyn went to Bath for the night before travelling on to Lynmouth where they spent their honeymoon, as their son Harold did after them.

William's firstborn was Maisie Rover who was born on 9 April 1911 followed by Wilfrid John in 1912. Their third child was Harold Gainsford.

With the marriage and the arrival of the children, William and his brother John together with their family friend William Buckland made plans for their future. William Buckland put up the capital for the brothers to set up a firm dealing in wadding and wool, in Bishopsgate in the City of London. They called the firm A. Allen as this would appear at the beginning of their customers' address book. However there was a long-term strategy, which was that once the firm was up and running, the younger brother William was to take over the management of Mr Buckland's farm in Wantage, Oxfordshire while John managed the London firm. The First World War changed all this as John Gainsford went to war and William ran the firm and continued to do so until he was well into his eighties.

Maisie Rover was their firstborn. She was a very happy little girl and enjoyed all the usual sporting pursuits, especially swimming, despite having to wear a woollen swimming costume. She went to Gowan Lee private school and when the family moved to Loughton she went to the Loughton High School at the bottom of the road. She was a popular student and made many friends whom she kept all her life. She left school at sixteen and lived at home helping her mother in the kitchen and garden where she became a splendid gardener. She also went with her mother to the weekly teas with Evelyn's sisters and also to William's sisters. The families were very close and kept well in touch. Weekends were also spent visiting at either William or Evelyn's parents with the children. These were very happy days for them all with their tennis parties and other pleasurable pursuits.

However by the late 1930s the world was becoming an increasingly dangerous place with the rise of Hitler in Germany and Mussolini in Italy. When it became inevitable that there would be another war, Maisie started nursing training at King George's Hospital at Newbury Park. She passed her training with flying colours and took up her work in the hospital wards. Here she nursed many soldiers and even helped out at many of the London hospitals.

When the war ended, she decided not to go back to her previous life and retrained as a Queen's Nurse, Midwife and District Nurse. At first, she was assigned to work in the East End of London, which she found rewarding though very hard work. In 1950, she decided to apply for a new position and started work in Battle, Sussex. She was given a nurse's house which was an old Tudor building with beams and low ceilings. It was in Mount Street near to the town centre. However with the increasing use of cars it became necessary to have a car and therefore a garage. The Nursing Association built two purpose built flats out of town next to the town playing fields with a good view of Battle Abbey. Maisie and her colleague Nurse Cook spent many years in these flats and Maisie made the garden really beautiful.

In the mid sixties, her brother Harold advised her to buy a property and she bought the lovely cottage at Mount Pleasant. Here she established yet another beautiful garden. She continued to work until her retirement caring for the sick and bringing many babies in to the world.

She was always very busy in her retirement with numerous family visitors and also with painting and carpentry. Tragically she was killed in a road accident on 18 August 1984 two days before she was to visit her niece Hazel in Australia.

Wilfrid John was born on 4 October 1912. He too was a very happy child and was, like his father, of a technical nature. He went with Maisie to Gowan Lee and then went to Forest School where Harold joined him and the two brothers were confirmed together in the school chapel. Despite the fact that the two boys had very different personalities they were good friends and did a great deal together. They both shared a love of the forest and nature. Although Harold was more studious and less active than Wilfrid they played lots of tennis together, and Wilfrid was often able to get Harold out of his chair to go off for a ramble. Wilfrid also helped his father a great deal around the house and garden, having the same practical temperament.

During his twenties Wilfrid devoted a great deal of his spare time to the work of Toc H. He was working by this time at A. Allen and company with his father.

He married Doris Hazeldine on 3 June 1939 on a sunny and warm afternoon at the Loughton Methodist Church and they started married life at 12 Roundmead Avenue,

Loughton. Their daughter Hazel was born on 21 January 1941. The family continued to live in Roundmead Avenue.

Wilfrid was a truly inspiring character. At the outbreak of war he joined the Royal Navy but very sadly was killed in an accident on 13 August 1944 on HMS *Excalibur* where he was serving just as his training for a commission was drawing to a close.

William and Evelyn bore the loss bravely but the sadness remained, especially around Remembrance time. Their lives continued to revolve around their family. They were frequent visitors at the home of William's sisters Annie and Dolly at Wanstead and Evelyn rarely missed the gathering of her sisters on a Wednesday afternoon. After the chat there was always a real Victorian tea served on the best Crown Derby tea service. Holidays were always taken at Eastbourne at Easter and at Cromer or Looe in the summer although in 1911 they spent their summer here at Felixstowe. The town had recently gained popularity by the visit of the German Empress in 1891.

The high spot of their year was Christmas, which was a typical Edwardian occasion. The meal was the traditional turkey and ham with all the trimmings. This was followed by home made Christmas pudding and mince pies, which had been made on 'Stir Up Sunday'. All were served with boiled egg custard. After the washing up and a little rest the celebrations continued with the Queen's speech. After this the presents were distributed before the children performed a play. Parlour games were then played before afternoon tea and Christmas cake was served. The family continued to play games like Consequences, 'Please we have come to act a trade' and Charades. At 7 p.m. a large supper with yet another Christmas pudding was served. Everyone then went to bed replete and very happy.

The couple celebrated their Golden Wedding in June 1960 at the Laurels with a happy family party, which was indeed a great celebratory occasion.

William and Evelyn were thrilled when their first two grandsons were born. Malcolm was born to Hazel and her husband John Cribb in Papua where they were working as missionaries. James the elder son of Judith and Ian Campbell was born on 2 June 1964 and the couple saw James baptized at St Mary's where Judith and Ian had been married, which delighted them. Afterwards there was a family tea party at the Wilrae Hotel with the top layer of the wedding cake being used as a christening cake for the baby.

Evelyn died on 10 March 1965 and William followed her on 6 April 1965.

CHAPTER 4

John Henry French
1855–1942

John Henry French was born at a time of unprecedented peace in Europe, the only exception being the Crimean War of 1854 to 1856. England was also increasing in material prosperity with its ever expanding industrial production and foreign trade. The railways were continuing to develop, as were the heavy industries such as Iron and Steel and the Shipbuilding business. Abroad there was also a buoyant mood, which also emphasized this materialism. However this was tempered with a strict religious faith with its belief in strict Sunday observance and its belief in self-improvement.

John Henry French was born at 22, Murray Street in Hoxton New Town London. He was the second son of John Gainsford French and his wife Emily and was named after his father and his father's last surviving brother. At the time, John Gainsford who was a fully qualified veterinarian surgeon was working as a railway clerk to support his family. However soon after John's birth he got a job as a vet. John's elder brother was named George and had been born on 17 April 1854 in Wharf Road just off the City Road in the Saint Luke's District of the City of London. His parents were living there at the time with friends of Emily whom she had met when she had lived at home with her parents in Woodford Essex. A year later, on 19 March, John and George were joined by another brother Richard Dixon, the latter name being the surname of John Gainsford's mother before her marriage. He too was born in Hoxton but at 132 High Street.

On 24 April 1861, John and Emily were living in Back Church Lane in Saint George's in the East. Here they had a little girl Kate who was her father's pride and joy. The family was made complete with the arrival of Gainsford William on 30 January 1864. The family had again moved to Eagle Wharf Road also in Hoxton New Town. This house was a very smart three bedroomed Victorian house and reflected the family's change in financial fortune.

By 1866 John Gainsford was sufficiently wealthy to be able to purchase 11 Groombridge Road Bethnal Green near to Victoria Park. This was an elegant four bedroomed Victorian property, which was situated in a quiet tree lined road. It was very smart with sash windows and had a very attractive brass door knocker.

John Henry was a very quiet, modest and retiring child and he did not change throughout his life in this respect. He is remembered as being a very kindly but quiet presence who remained in the background at all the family events He left school at fourteen and by the age of fifteen was established at work as a commercial clerk. He remained a clerk thoughout his working life working also as broker's clerk as well as colonial clerk.

In 1871, John was still living in the family home in Groombridge Road. However in 1874, his father died and his mother together with the two younger children moved to a smaller home and John went into lodgings at 147 Junction Road, Islington.

While he was living there he met his future wife, Annie Hall. Annie was a lively and very cheerful young lady and was the third daughter of Richard and Mary Ann Hall. Richard was an India rubber maker but he had died

before the young couple met. On 10 October 1875 John
and Ann were married at Saint Mary's Parish Church in
Islington.

They moved to rooms in a lovely Victorian house at
13 Francis Terrace, which were just round the corner
from Annie's mother's home. Here their first child Annie
Isabella was born on 4 October 1876.

The family then increased in size and with the birth of
each new baby they moved as well. In 1878, Kate Julia
was born in Wigrams Lane Leytonstone and in 1880, John
Gainsford joined her. The family was by then living in
Caxton Road, Bow.

Willian Henry was born in Cobden Road Leytonstone
in 1881 and was followed by Agnes in 1883, Gainsford
in 1884 and Emily in 1886. The last child to be born was
Dorothy in 1889 and the family had by then moved to
Cann Hall Road Wanstead.

John's mother died on 9 September 1892 and John was
able to purchase a pleasant but modest home for his large
family at 5 Addison Road also in Wanstead with his
legacy under the terms of his late father's will.

Wanstead was a very pleasant place for the family to
live and was surrounded on all sides by forestland and
open spaces such as Wanstead Park and Wanstead Flats
with its beautiful lake and colony of herons. The former
was beautifully laid out by Richard Child the first Earl
Tylney.

Addison Road was situated just off the High Road with
its eighteenth century shops, which were interspersed with
new ones. It was also very near to the classical building
of Christ Church where all the children were baptized
and John and Annie were buried.

Annie Isabella was very like her father in temperament,
being quiet and gentle. She always lived at home and

helped her mother with the growing demands of the family, as most eldest daughters did in Victorian times. She was also, like her mother, an excellent cook and homemaker.

Kate Julia, who was William Henry's favourite sister and known as Katie, was born on the 24 April 1878. She was not like the rest of the family who were all very healthy. For years she suffered ill health but on 25 July 1903, she married Albert Ernest Brown who like his father before him was a mariner. For a while they lived near to the family home in Wanstead but in an attempt to improve Katie's health, Albert took her to Durban in South Africa. There they had their only child Katherine who was always known as Kitty. However the family returned to England in 1909 and when the Great War broke out, Albert took secondment from the Merchant Navy and joined the Royal Navy where he saw active service. He was at the Battle of Jutland, amongst other battles. After Albert's death Katie and Kitty lived with John and Annie in Addison Road. Kitty married Leonard Marsh. After her marriage she and her husband lived in the Uplands, in Loughton. The couple had two sons, Dennis and Peter.

Katie's brother, John Gainsford worked in the City of London, after leaving school as a clerk. At the outbreak of the Boer War in 1898, he enlisted in the City of London Imperial Volunteers as a private at their headquarters at James Street, Buckingham Gate. The CIV had been established when the War was going very badly when the then Lord Mayor of London Sir Alfred Newton had suggested to the Lord Wolsey the C in C that London should provide a regiment, drawn from a Volunteer force at the expense of the City. The whole operation was financed from the Livery Companies, City Businesses and private individuals. This regiment was in fact a

predecessor of the TA. John was assigned to the 13th
Middlesex Regiment which was normally referred to as
the 'Queen's Westminsters'. Together with many of his
friends he was put in Number 1 Company of the CIV
Mounted Infantry. He set sail for South Africa on *The
Briton* on the 13 January 1900 together with 450 other
men. As *The Times* of the day wrote there was plenty
of room for the 250 men to sleep on hammocks. The
Government also laid down the ration allowance and the
men lived in the style of third class passengers on a liner.
On a typical day their bill of fare was porridge, bloaters
and grilled mutton together with tea or coffee for
breakfast. The men were given soup on alternate days
for dinner, followed by roast beef or pork with pease
pudding and two vegetables. This was followed by a
sweet or cheese and biscuits. If they did not want this
hot dinner there was always cold meat and pickles as
well as bread and jam. In the evening they were given
cheese and biscuits and tea. All intoxicants were however
forbidden. Despite the comforting tone of *The Times'*
report, the voyage was not a pleasant one as there was
very little to do on board ship except to read, write or
sleep. They finally arrived in Cape Town on 29 January.

By 15 of February the Number 1 company had their
first engagement when they chased the Boers out of
Jacobsdaal near Kimberley. One of John's company noted
at the end of the engagement that all the men including
John enjoyed the tinned milk, jam and limejuice which
they obtained from the town. The company then became
involved in numerous engagements either as a complete
company or in ever changing detachments. As John was
only a private soldier they were rarely mentioned in
despatches. However there is one reference to him as
'serving temporarily with Brabant's Colonial Division,

most probably as a dispatch rider.'

At the end of hostilities, John, unlike many of his friends who had died of dysentery, survived the rigours of the heat and flies of South Africa. Before leaving South Africa the whole regiment held a parade and marched past Lord Roberts in Pretoria: this was the only time they all paraded together. The regiment then left Cape Town on 2 October 1900.

The journey was delayed by very bad weather and they only reached Southampton on the 29th. On the train to Paddington each soldier found a pork pie and a packet of stamps with a pencil, being a gift from Raphael Tuck and Company, under the seat. John then attended the march from Paddington Station to Saint Paul's Cathedral where there was a Service of Thanksgiving. There were enormous crowds on the streets of London and the soldiers individually had to fight their way through these crowds rather than marching together. After the service, the regiment then proceeded to Bunhill Fields where they were entertained to a vast homecoming dinner with their families. When the meal was finished each soldier handed in his rifle and bayonet in exchange for a silver topped swagger stick.

John was awarded the Queen's South African Medal with clasps for Driefontein, Paardeburg and Cape Colony. He received this medal from King Edward the Seventh on Horse Guards Parade in July 1901. He was also made a Freeman of the City of London for his services in CIV.

John then returned to his former employment before becoming a commercial traveller. Whilst pursuing this career he met his future wife Agnes Emily Fortescue in Bournemouth. They were married on 11 August 1903 at Saint Peter's Parish Church. The couple settled down at 15 Eastwood Road South Woodford Essex and had two daughters, Violet and Margaret. Violet went into business and Margaret became a Deaconess in the Church of England.

After the outbreak of the Great War, in 1915 John enlisted as a Sergeant with the Queen's Westminster Rifles and joined the Regular Army the next day being the 3 December. He was then posted to Number 3 Company where he was promoted to Lance Corporal on 4 July 1916 and again to Acting Sergeant Instructor three days later. On the 26 January 1918, he was attached to the Reserve Battalion of the Honourable Artillery Company and left Southampton on SS *Viper* for Cherbourg where he joined the SS *Marwa* en route for Basra. He arrived in Basra in Mesopotamia in February 1918 and returned to UK on 20 November 1918 after he had taken part in the Mesopotamia Expeditionary Force's campaign. For his services to the Crown, John was awarded both the British War Medal and the Victory Medal.

John had greatly enjoyed life in the Army and found life as a civilian rather tame. He was a very remote man and after the war he and his family went and lived in Bournmouth and had very little contact with the other members of the French family who remained very close indeed. He died on 10 December 1951.

Emily had gone to work in the office at Tate and Lyle and on 10 September 1910 she married Arthur Edward Lyons at Christ Church Wanstead. Emily was attended by her sisters Agnes and Dorothy and her nieces, Violet the daughter of John Gainsford and Katie's daughter Kitty. Arthur was the son of Francis Henry Lyons a jeweller from Cardiff and his wife and was a prominent member of the Leytonstone Rugby Football Club being not only a player but also the Honorary Secretary. The family joined Emily's brother William's family and his sisters for many very enjoyable holidays over the years and these were much enlivened by the presence of their daughter Stella who was somewhat of a madcap.

Arthur was a clerk and the couple also had a son Geoffrey as well as Stella. They lived at 52 Spring Grove, Loughton.

Agnes was the last sister to be married and she, to the delight of her brother William, married Harry Hancock on 6 July 1912 at Christ Church. Until her marriage, Agnes had also worked for Tate and Lyle. As well as being a good friend of William, Harry was a well-known chorister at Christ Church. For her wedding Agnes wore her mother in law's veil and orange blossom. She was attended by her sister Dorothy and John Gainsford's daughter Violet. The couple had one daughter Bettina and they lived also in Spring Grove, Loughton.

Dorothy continued to live at home and work for Tate and Lyle until her retirement.

The extended family continued to have holidays together for many years and met weekly for tea or for the day.

John Henry's wife Annie was a wonderful cook and made really mouth-watering gingerbread. She was unfailingly cheerful and loved to have her grandchildren around her and played many games with them. They in their turn loved her very much.

Very sadly Annie got cancer and died in March 1929. John Henry continued to live with his daughters Annie and Dolly at Addison Road and life continued in its customary way with family visits to Wanstead and trips out to Loughton to see all the members of his family. He was really delighted when his grandson Harold had a daughter Judith and he was able to enjoy her for the last year of his life. He died on 26 January 1942. Both he and his wife were buried in the graveyard of Christ Church Wanstead. The sisters Annie and Dolly continued to live together at what all the family called Number 5. After Annie died in November 1961, Dolly continued to live in the house for ten more years until she herself moved to Loughton to an Abbeyfield Home in the High Road as her sight was failing. She lived to a month short of her hundredth birthday.

CHAPTER 5

John Gainsford French 1809–1874

John Gainsford was born into a war-torn world with the Napoleonic War drawing to its close. England was still a predominantly agricultural country and even in London, families were mostly country bred. However as the years after 1815 passed, the Industrial Revolution was revving up in the North which brought with it a rapidly changing pace of life. The population grew and the country's wealth also increased dramatically. With the now diminishing power of George III, Parliament's power increased. In 1832 the Great Reform Bill was passed which increased the franchise by 217,000 men to all owners of ten pound properties as well as to copyholders and leaseholders. This directly affected the French family, as John Gainsford was a copyholder of property in Chelmsford. Copyhold was a manorial term and was similar to freehold except when the tenant died the property was transferred to the Lord of the Manor who in his turn returned it to the heir.

Although materialism was general among the population there was also a new feeling of liberalism abroad amongst the thinking men, which was influenced by such men as Jeremy Bentham, who believed in trying to bring the greatest happiness to the greatest number of people. In fact this way of thought not only achieved the status of a national philosophy but also became the national policy as it provided the principles whereby there was an orderly transition to the complete freedom of industry and the enfranchisement of the middle classes. By the end of John Gainsford's life, England had also made a small start in sorting out the slums and the bad conditions in the factories and the mines.

As the century passed, food became very expensive with the run of bad harvests and the consequent high price of corn. This caused widespread unrest and resulted in the Factory Acts and the subsequent Repeal of the Corn Laws. The new thinking was further influenced by the combined good works of men such as Lord Shaftesbury and John Stewart Mill as well as the Chartist Movement and the consequent establishment of the Trade Union movement. All these factors changed the people's way of life forever.

Until I started my research into the French Family, John Gainsford French was a shadowy figure in the past. William Henry and his sister Annie who had both dabbled in genealogy had heard vague stories that he was a six-foot vet. However they believed this to be a myth although they did think he could have been a self appointed horse vet. He was, in fact, a highly intelligent man with many independent opinions. I also think from studying his life and papers that he could have been a difficult man to live with as he was very ambitious and also wanted to improve his financial and social position constantly. However although he was very successful in both these projects, his sons do not seem to have wanted to talk about him which rather suggests a remote man, although he did die when they were fairly young so their memories could be hazy. Also he did not marry their mother until they were teenagers and was very secretive on this matter. He was in fact a typical example of the self-made man in the Victorian era and could well have espoused the theories put forward by Samuel Smiles in 1859. These in essence were that the virtues of hard work and honesty brought great rewards of material prosperity. He and his grandfather were certainly the most fascinating of the men of the French family in the eighteenth and nineteenth centuries.

John Gainsford French was born on 31 October 1809 in Springfield Lane, Chelmsford in Essex and was baptized on 18 November of the same year at Saint Mary's Church in the town. He was the eldest son of John French a Coach Proprietor and his wife Sarah. Sarah was the daughter of Gainsford Dixon the owner of the Queen's Head Inn on the High Street who was a very good friend and colleague of John Gainsford's grandfather. It is from Gainsford Dixon that this name entered the French Family where it has continued for 150 years with my son Jonathan also having this name.

John and Sarah had a very large number of children, most of whom did not survive infancy. George who was born on 23 June 1811 lived until 17 December 1835 and all his sisters predeceased their mother Sarah; all succumbing to the scourge of consumption. The one son other than John Gainsford who survived his parents was Henry who was born on 30 December 1828 and lived until old age like John.

John was most probably educated at the King Edward's School in Chelmsford and on 28 August 1824, he entered the Royal Veterinary College in London.*

The Royal Veterinary College London had evolved from the London Committee of the Oldham Agricultural Society, which was a group of men drawn from

---

* Register of the Royal Veterinary College 1824

'Gentleman of rank, fortune and integrity – and intelligent farmers.' One of them was a Thomas Burgess who decided to 'campaign for a more humane treatment of sick animals' focusing his attention on farriery. The College was later responsible for many considerable advances in both veterinary and other related sciences. The first professor at the College was a Frenchman Charles Vial de St Penn. When John Gainsford attended the College, Edward Coleman was one of the joint professors who ran the College. He had been considered to be a very controversial choice as he not only lowered the standards of entry to the College but also allowed the medical profession to exert too much influence on College affairs. He also shortened the length of the courses and concentrated on the teaching of one species – namely the horse. However he did increase the social standing of the position of the veterinary surgeon. Both these latter influences worked very well for John Gainsford.

John is on the register as attending all the lectures and lived in Islington and qualified with their Diploma on 12 July 1830. By 1842, he is listed as either a Governor or Officer of the College and is shown as practising as a vet in Chelmsford.*

On 9 September 1835, John Gainsford's father John died. It seems highly probable that the cause of death was consumption, which was also the cause of his son George's death three months later.

John left £2,000 in his will and under its terms both John and George inherited all their father's share in the Coaching Company of French and Woods as well as all his share in the profits. This consisted of all the coaches, the black coach and the hearse as well as all the harness,

---

*   The Journal of the Royal College of Veterinarians 1830 and 1874

corn and feed. This was given on the condition that they paid their mother two guineas a week for life. She was left all her husband's property in Springfield Lane and all his furniture and plate.

On the death of George, John Gainsford ran the coaching company with his mother Sarah. From 1826, his father John French had introduced his newly patented Long Coaches, which accommodated four inside passengers and from eight to eleven passengers outside. By this time the company ran a daily service and the journey started on alternate days from either The Spread Eagle in Gracechurch Street in the City of London at 7.45 a.m., 9.45 a.m. and 3.45 p.m. or from The Green Dragon in Bishopsgate at 9.45 a.m. and 7.30 p.m. The Company had also been running a similar service from The Spread Eagle in Piccadilly but this was stopped, as it was not considered to be economic.* The journey then proceeded through Romford, Brentwood and Ingatestone to the Ship Inn at Chelmsford, which John French the elder owned. The business was extremely successful and continued to prosper until the arrival of the steam trains from London.

In 1837, John Gainsford took a fourth share in the Ship Inn with his grandfather John, Charles George Parker of Springfield Place, a family friend and Henry Woods of Aldersgate Street London the son of William who had established the company with John French the elder many years before.

On 12 June 1840, John appeared before the Court of the Bishop of London in order to obtain a Marriage Licence to marry Sarah Quinn at Saint Mary's Church Islington.** The couple were married three days later with

*   Boyds Directory for Chelmsford
**   Licence held in the Palace of Lambeth Library

the witnesses being John's two good friends, William Dawson and Joseph Robert. Sarah was the daughter of James Quinn a farmer of Chelmsford and it is more than probable that John met her when he was working as a vet in the town. They chose Saint Mary's Church for their wedding as it was very near where John had studied at the Veterinary College in Camden Town.

After the wedding, the couple settled down to married life in Chelmsford. They lived in a house on the High Street, which was only a few doors away from The Ship Inn. The young couple also looked after John's younger brother Henry who was fifteen at the time.

However 1840 changed from a happy year into a very grim one for John Gainsford. His grandfather died on 12 May at the great age of 80 and his Uncle George who ran the branch of French and Woods from Malden to Chelmsford also died on 7 August of the same year.

As a result of these events, John Gainsford set off to Malden with his wife Sarah to assist his aunt in the running of that branch of the Company leaving his mother to run the Chelmsford to London coach service on her own. His aunts who had been left the Ship Inn in their father's will then ran it and carried on for the next thirty years.

In 1842, John's Aunt Ann in Malden also died and in 1843 John who had been living in the town and working very hard decided to sell his quarter share in the Ship Inn for £340 to his aunts Rebecca and Isabella. His cousin George Anthony then took over the running of the wagon business in late 1843 under the terms of his late father's will and John Gainsford and Sarah decided to move to London to seek their fortune there.

At this time, London was a rapidly changing city and by the mid-1800s gaslights were appearing on the streets and steam vessels would soon be plying their trade on the River Thames. Also both omnibuses and hansom cabs appeared on all the London streets and new shops were opening such as Lilley and Skinner and Swan and Edgar. Many of the old houses were demolished to make way for the road improvement schemes but these never kept pace with the ever-increasing traffic.

Fashions changed for men like John Gainsford and they started to wear dull and sombre clothes and have moustaches, which for many years William Henry sported, as well as side-whiskers. Also the only jewellery men now wore were rings and cufflinks and watches on chains. A new philosophy was also abroad in that the reward of virtue was great wealth and influence. In fact the Victorian Man believed that the mark of the favour of God was prosperity. For the next fifty years these men believed themselves to be one of the chosen race and this view filled them with a certain degree of self confidence and in some case smugness and arrogance.

Religion also played a very large part in family life during these years with families attending church three times a day on Sunday and having daily prayers at home as William Henry later told me he had done. This led people to develop a genuine and deep concern for the conditions of the poor, which are shown in the Acts of Parliament of the time, which were made to protect children and lunatics as well as prohibiting the employment of children as chimneysweeps.

It was against this background that John and Sarah discovered that life in London was not as easy for them as John had expected. With his qualifications he had expected that to get a job as a vet would be comparatively easy but sadly this did not happen. However he did get work as a coachmaster and so he and Sarah took lodgings in the City at North Lodgings, Finsbury.

Sadly Sarah died on 6 October 1849 of consumption and John was left a widower.

He continued to work in London and live in the City and he would have been consoled his two friends William Dawson and Joseph Robert. However life for him was soon to change forever. While he was living in North Buildings in Finsbury he made the acquaintance of a young mother of two small children Edward James and Emily Sarah. Her name was Emily Pearce and she had been born in Chingford in Essex on 19 October 1823. She was the daughter of a builder Thomas Lowe and his wife Sarah. The family lived in Woodford in Essex like John and so the couple had this County in common. Emily was married to Henry Daniel Pearce who was a proprietor of houses and most probably John Gainsford had met him about renting a place in which to live. It obviously became apparent that the couple were attracted to each other and after three years they fell in love. At this time the only way that a couple could get a divorce was by a Private Member's Bill in the House of Lords, which was not a process that the ordinary man could adopt, being so costly. As a result they set up home as man and wife without a divorce.

Not long after this Henry Pearce moved to Woodford where he lived with his 74-year old landlady, Elizabeth Rutherford in the house, which was next door to his wife's brother, until his death on 6 December 1867. He was buried in the Parish Church in Woodford. This whole episode in the history of the French family seems very bizarre as they were so religious, but was not however contrary to the customs of the time.

By 1854, the young couple had moved in with Emily's friend Sarah whom she had known since their childhood in Woodford. Sarah was herself married to Thomas Sprules who was a soda water maker and they lived at 28 Wharf Road in the Saint Luke district of the City of London. On 17 April Emily had her first child with John Gainsford and they called him after John's brother George who had died in 1835.

Later George was baptized on April 1863, at St Leonard's Church Shoreditch, with his two brothers and one sister.

George trained to be a clerk and after the death of his father he left home and took up lodgings at 3 Trafalgar Road in Haggerston. After about a year, he met Isabella Amelia, the daughter of a local solicitor William Henry Gillard and his wife Lavinia. George was doing very well in his work and had become the local manager of the London General Omnibus Company. On 22 September 1875 at the age of twenty-two, the young people got married at Saint Mary's the Parish Church of Haggerston. Richard and Gainsford as well as Kate attended the wedding. Their first child was a girl who they named Isabella Kate. She was followed by a boy who was born on in 1877 and was named George Gainsford Henry.

George was by this time the superintendent of the London General Omnibus Company in the area and the family was living at 73 Cricketfeld Road in Hackney, which was a three storey Victorian house together with an area as well. They had to climb up a steep set of steps to the front door with its pillars and inset door. George's father in law who was by this time 63 years old lived with them after the death of his wife together with his daughter Marion who was only fourteen years old at the time. George and Isabella had moved from a much smaller home in Elderfield Road, which was also in Hackney. Another little boy was born on 18 October 1885,

Gainsford Frederick George, who died at birth. During this time, George became a Mason and was a member of the Duke of Connaught's Lodge.

Isabella Amelia died on 13 December 1903 from emphysema and bronchitis. The next year George Gainsford who was an omnibus driver for the London Omnibus Company married Elizabeth Sharp. She was a lovely girl and the daughter of the late William Sharp a clerk. They were married at the Parish Church in Hackney on the 7 September 1904. George and Elizabeth were a devoted couple and Elizabeth on his rest days from work would never allow any callers as she preferred to keep her husband to herself.

The couple had five daughters Hilda, Doris, Violet, Lilian and Mabel. Their only son George Gainsford Frederick died at the age of five on 4 November 1911 after suffocating from a piece of meat which had got stuck in his throat. I was in touch for many years with the youngest daughter Mabel who was a lovely person and a mine of information about her branch of the family as was her very kind niece Daphne, Hilda's daughter.

Richard Dixon was the third son of John Gainsford and Emily. He was born on 19 March 1857 at 132 High Street Hoxton and baptized later with George at Saint Leonard's Church. After the death of his father, he also left home and set up home in Stepney where he was working as a clerk and later as the manager of a bedding company. On 3 January 1880, he married Alice Catherine Edwards the daughter of James the local Parish Clerk. Emily, Kate and Gainsford attended the marriage and the couple settled down into married life at 18 Broomhead Street in Mile End Old Town. His mother Emily lived just along the road with the two younger children and her daughter Emily Sidebotham by Henry Pearce who was also a widow. Richard and Alice had three children, Florence Kate born on 15 January 1881, Nellie Beatrice born on 13 February 1886 and Richard John born in 1888.

Richard John was a very tall, quiet and calm man and was in fact very like John Henry French. He worked until 1926 when a heart condition, which he had sustained during the Great War, caused him to stop. His wife came from East Bergholt and they lived for part of their lives in Wood Green before moving to Worcester Park. They had one son Richard. Richard married Rhoda Margaret Rees in April 1941. They lived for five years in Greenford when they moved to Southgate where their two children were born. The elder was Martin Andrew who was born in 1942 and their daughter Jill Annette who was born in 1946.

Richard and Alice moved out to Tottenham before the birth of Nellie and the family stayed in this area of London for the next fifty years. Alice died at home on the first of December 1888 of consumption, and after her death, Richard and the children went to live with his mother Emily at 121 Godwin Road in Forest Gate, West Ham. Here he helped his brother Gainsford William as a fruiterer at the family shop. However when his mother died, Richard and his children moved to 29 Beaulay Road Tottenham and his sister in law Charlotte Edwards who had helped him with his wife's last illness moved in to care for the children and housekeep for the family. Richard also took in lodgers to supplement his income as a law stationer. He worked with twelve other law writers who were under him. He continued with the firm until the advent of the typewriter, which caused the demise of the business.* One of Richard's lodgers was John Hardy,

---

* Information provided by Mr Martin French, Great Grandson

a stone mason, who married Florence Kate on 31 May 1903 at Tottenham Parish Church.

Gainsford William was the youngest son of John and Emily and he lived with his mother until the age of 18. He was apprenticed to a tailor in Mile End at the age of fourteen and continued to work in this trade until he realized that this was not the right job for him.

Gainsford was a very active young man and like his father had a great love of horses and so he decided to join the Royal Scots Greys as a dragoon. He was quickly promoted first to Lance Corporal and then to Corporal and subsequently reached the rank of Sergeant. He had an exemplary service record for which he was paid 183 shillings for 5 months service with 183 pence for Good Conduct pay. Whilst he was serving at Aldershot he married Mary Conway the daughter of Owen Conway, a House Agent, on 8 July 1886 at the Saint Francis de Sales Chapel in Edmonton. All the family joined in the celebrations before the young couple were posted to Dundalk Ireland where their first child, a daughter Winifred Emily, was born in Barrack Street on 16 February 1889. In 1890, Gainsford left the army and the family returned to England. They settled in Bromley by Bow and Gainsford quickly got a job as an omnibus driver as he had been riding for years with the Royal Scots Greys. The couple's second daughter Kate Agnes was born on 21 September 1890.

However by this time, Gainsford's mother, Emily, who was 68 years old was finding that the running of her greengrocery store was becoming too onerous. She had bought the business together with a large flat above the shop with her inheritance from her husband. Also Richard who had lost his wife needed someone to care for his young children. After a family conference it was decided that Richard should give up his managerial job and work with his mother. They also decided that it made more sense for both the two brothers to work together as fruiterers and live above the shop in the ample accommodation, so Gainsford and his family also went to live in Godwin Road, West Ham. Thus not only were there Emily's two sons by John Gainsford living in the house together with their families but also her widowed daughter Emily Sidebotham. The latter did not help in the shop but continued to work as a furrier and bring money into the household.

On 9 August 1992, Emily died suddenly of a heart attack, and was buried with John Gainsford in Abney Park Cemetery. After her death the shop had to be sold under the terms of John Gainsford's Will and the monies divided between the children. Gainsford moved back to Bow and bought a house at 60 Ettrick Street. He took up his work again as a stagecoach driver. He and his wife lived together very happily and had four more children, Owen John in 1894, George William in 1896 and Bernard in 1900. Sadly their son John Gainsford who was born in 1892 died in 1895. Bernard was fondly remembered by his Uncle George's granddaughter Mabel, especially when he went off to the Great War. He stayed with George before going overseas and on his return from Service in Egypt, he gave pretty bead necklaces to all of George's granddaughters.

When Mary, his wife died, Gainsford went to live with George and his son George at the home that the former had bought with his inheritance money at 50 Salcombe Road, Leyton. Gainsford was a lovely man and was very kind not only to his own children but also to George's son and his young family who all treasure happy memories of him.

Gainsford easily made the transition from being a horse driven omnibus driver to that of being a motor bus driver. He continued in this work until 26 April 1920 when he suffered a cerebral haemorrhage at George's house. He was a bit tired when he got home from work and after eating his dinner went upstairs for a nap. Elizabeth, Gainsford George's wife took him a cup of tea about an hour later and found him unconscious in the bed. There was of course an inquest. His superior and his work colleagues told the Court that he had been fine at work until 2 p.m. but suddenly felt very giddy. Elizabeth later found that he had been sick in the bed and was by then unconscious. He died very soon afterwards. The cause of death after a post-mortem examination was deemed to be coma and cerebral haemorrhage. He was only 56 years old.

Finally we come to John and Emily's daughter Kate, who was born on 24 April 1863. By all accounts she was not only very pretty but she was also very lively. Furthermore she was the apple of her father's eye. He was a typically remote father with all his sons but with Kate he was completely different and really quite spoilt her.

She enjoyed this attention and was very upset at his early death. After this and while John Gainsford's estate was being sorted out, Emily and the two youngest children moved in with Emily's widowed daughter Emily in Broomhead Street in Mile End Old Town. It was here in the East End that Kate fell in love with James Lowe her husband to be who was also her cousin, being her mother's nephew.

James was the youngest son of Emily's eldest brother Thomas. He and Emily had been brought up firstly in Chingford and later at Walnut Tree Cottage Inman Row, just next to the Church at Woodford Wells in Essex.

James had been educated at the Board School in Woodford and at the age of fourteen he went to work for the local grocer and corn dealer. When he was seventeen he joined the staff of the General Post Office as a sorter. While he was working for the post office he also became a Rifle Volunteer for 13 months.* He soon decided that the life in the Post Office was very dull and not nearly active enough for him and he applied for a situation as a Police Constable with the City of London Police. He was accepted and joined the service on 20 August 1877 as a constable. His pay was 25 shillings a week and he was stationed at Seething Lane Police Station. He remained in the Police Force until his retirement in 1902.

James was 5 feet 10 inches tall with dark brown eyes and hair and from his service record was a bit of a lad. A year after he joined he had to forfeit a day's pay for gossiping and idling with a female. This pattern of behaviour continued and he received persistent forfeitures from his pay for talking to girls and idling in Public Houses. For the latter behaviour he had to promise to reform otherwise he would be dismissed.**

He lived in Police accommodation just round the corner from his Aunt Emily and her daughter Kate. Kate was very like him in temperament as they were both live wires. They soon decided to get married and all the family joined the wedding ceremony at Saint Thomas Church in Arbour Square in Stepney. James kept out of mischief for a couple of years and then he was back to his old tricks of drinking in a wine cellar whilst on duty. Kate was also not a very good housewife as his promotion to first class was retarded because his uniform was in holes at a general inspection. The couple lived at 52 Duke Street

---

*   Declaration for an application for service in the City of London police
** Service Record City of London Police

in Aldgate and there they had their first child on 20 June 1883. They called her Florence Kate Emily. They had a son Thomas Gainsford on 6 January 1885 but sadly he died within twelve hours. The young couple were obviously in an impecunious state as the baby was buried in a common grave in the East London cemetery at Plaistow.*

The family had by then moved to 52 Myrdle Street in Mile End Old Town and on 31 August 1893, Kate died of chronic nephritis albumensis. James continued to work in London for the City of London Police and live in the Police house at the Minories in Aldgate until his retirement.

Meanwhile his daughter Florence went to live with her Grandmother Emily and after her death went to Woodford to live with Emily's brother Thomas. When she was fourteen she was apprenticed to her Aunt Mary Ann Ellen Lowe as a trainee dressmaker and by the age of 17 was an assistant dressmaker.

On January 20 1908 Florence married Archibald Ernest Cameron Robertson at Brixham Parish Church. James, her father had retired from the Police in 1902, and had moved to Brixham in Devonshire where he owned a house he called Woodford after his old home village where he grew up as a child. James died at the age of 90 at Kohat Collaton in Paignton on 16 April 1951 and Florence followed him at her home Summer Lea, Brixham on 13 August 1960.

In 1866, after the birth of their five children John Gainsford and Emily decided to buy a new house which had just been built in Groombridge Road the year before. By this time John was the Manager of the London General

---

* Cemetery Records East of London Cemetery, Grange Road, Plaistow

Omnibus Company in Bell Lane.* He had certainly made
a great deal of progress careerwise over the twelve years
he and Emily had been together. He had worked for a
while as an omnibus driver although he was a coachmaster
by profession. He had then had a spell as a railway clerk
but by 1857, he was working in the East End of London
as a veterinary surgeon, which would have both helped
his self-esteem and his financial situation. However by
1866 when he took out the indenture in order to buy his
new home his position was given as a gentleman. He had
also inherited a considerable amount of money from his
Aunt Isabella in 1865 and this enabled him to purchase
the lease on his new home on 11 May 1866. The family
was living at the time at Downhills Farm in Tottenham
as denoted on the indenture by which he bought the lease
on his new home. This lease covered all the outbuildings,
garden walls and iron railings. The house was situated
on the north side of the road, which was in the Parish
of Saint John's in Hackney. The lease was for 90 years
and John immediately got a mortgage on the property
with the Planet Benefit Buildings and Investment Society
for the same 90 years.** The garden was some sixty foot
long and backed on to a common. Groombridge Road
was also laid out with trees on both sides of the road
and the Church of Saint John's was at the top of the
road. It was a very pleasant place for the family to live
and it is interesting to note that even after 135 years, it
still has retained its traditional values and changed very
little. In fact the only thing that had changed even allowing
for inflation was the value of the property. The house

---

*   Court Directory 1870
**   Indenture Number 872 Martin to French 9 May 1866 and 873 French
     to Planet

was valued in 1999 at £325,000.

Life changed for the better in 1867 when Emily's husband Daniel died and in the Post Office and the Court Directories of that year John is listed. However the couple did not get married until the elder two boys were at work as clerks. They went to the Holborn Register Office to be married quietly with only Emily's childhood friend Sarah Sprules and her husband Thomas on 13 March 1872 in attendance.

Everything was now established in an orderly fashion and in keeping with Victorian values. George and John were starting out in their adult life and there were only Richard, Gainsford and Kate, who were at school, living at home full time. The family also had two general servants to help Emily so after the hard times the good times were starting to roll. John still owned the houses which had belonged to his father in Springfield Lane Chelmsford which provided him with their rent. This also entitled him to vote in the Essex Elections as the houses were held under the ancient land tenure custom of Copyhold.*

This custom decreed that a property held by someone who was a 'manorial tenant' was said to be copyhold. Their tenancy rights were set out in a copy of an entry on the court rolls of the Lord of the Manor who held them. These rights were given at a ceremony of admission, which took place either at a full sitting of the court or privately in a solicitor's office. This copy and the entry on the roll were the only evidence the tenant had of his entitlement, and were made by the clerks or the steward who compiled the minutes. They were then strapped into the front of their conveyance with the court rolls.

* Electoral Register 1875 for Chelmsford

Copyhold could be entailed, which could only be broken by surrendering the property to the 'will of the Lord'. There was in fact very little difference between holding a freehold or a copyhold property as the latter could be sub let for a maximum of 3 years, mortgaged, bequeathed or be sold.

However by early 1874 John Gainsford became ill from a softening of the spine and he died on 29 September. On 3 October 1874 his death was announced in the Saturday edition of *The Hackney Guardian*. It was also announced in *The Veterinarian* the yearly publication of the Royal College of Veterinarians, that Mr John French MRCVS of Chelmsford had died.* Emily bought a grave for her husband in Abney Park Cemetery where he was laid to rest.**

By the beginning of September of 1874, he knew he was dying and so he made a very long and comprehensive will. This document shows that his house was obviously very well furnished with much fine furniture and many good paintings. It also had a great deal of silver plated items, ornaments, books and prints. All these items were left to Emily, as was the equipment in the outhouses together with his horses and carriages. He had also leased the Down Hills farm, which was similarly furnished. All these items were also left to Emily.

He further instructed his executors to sell the London properties together with the copyhold houses in Chelmsford and give the proceeds to Emily. The Ship Inn at Chelmsford was however left to his daughter Kate. (He seemed to have forgotten that he had sold his share in 1843). It is of interest to note that Emily is described

---

*   The Royal Veterinarian February 1875 Volume III 614
**   The Register of Burials, Abney Park, Square 64 grave 55183

as late Pearce and not Lowe, so he was admitting the fact of her previous marriage to the world.

He then instructed that his two friends William and Joseph Dawson were to be his executors. As well as the property, John had a great deal of stock funds and securities, the interest of which Emily was to use for the upkeep of his five children rather than him setting up a separate trust for each of them. If however Emily remarried or when she died these properties and the securities were left to the children in equal parts with the proviso aforementioned that the Ship should go to his favourite Kate.

The probate value of John's estate was originally set at four thousand pounds.

John's two executors were both tobacconists who worked near the Bell Yard in Bell Lane where he worked. Also John called in a loan of four hundred pounds which he had made to Maria Elizabeth Gill, the landlady of the Cork and Hop of Gun Lane which was near his offices in Spitalfields. He wanted this money to be collected at all speed so that his widow would not be inconvenienced. From this one can assume that John was not only a smoker and drinker but also enjoyed the friendly atmosphere of a public house. He also could have been a bit of a lady's man as he had helped out a lady in financial distress! So his Will also gives us a further understanding of the character of the man who was John Gainsford French.

CHAPTER 6

John French
1786–1835

England had experienced a time of great social upheaval and change both in industry and in agriculture during the eighteenth century. This greatly changed the lives of everyone in the land. There was also a great increase in the population, which was in the main the result of a general fall in the death rate. The number of plagues and similar epidemics had fallen which had been brought about by the seventeenth century practice of burying the dead in coffins combined with the discovery of a vaccination against small pox. This, together with the establishment of maternity hospitals had helped to overcome many of the problems of infant and maternal deaths. Further the use of winter fodder for cattle also had made fresh meat and milk more readily available and with the coming of the railways, this food was able to get to the towns more easily. All these factors taken together generally improved the standard of living of the population.

The eighteenth century also saw the biggest rise in numbers in the middle classes with their gradual expansion into commerce combined with the general increase in trade. This enabled them to break through the aristocratic and land-owning monopoly of the government of the county by the increase in manhood suffrage.

All these trends benefited John French who was born

in Sudbury on 26 November 1786 and his life was to be greatly influenced by all these changes.

He was the third child of John and Ann French who lived in Sudbury. John was baptized at Saint Peter's Church in the town. At the time of John's birth, his father was working as a victualler for his Uncle Samuel who was a grocer in Sudbury. He also worked for his cousin Anthony who was a baker. Prior to this he had been a weaver. However the weaving trade and life in general in Sudbury was at very low ebb. The town had also been suffering from the putrid fever, which was most probably caused by its proximity to the River Stour. which ran through the town. In fact John's sister Sarah, who was born two years before him, died the year after his birth and the likely cause was the fever. This caused so much grief to his parents that they decided that they would have to move away and seek their fortune elsewhere.

Thus two years after John's birth, the family moved to Colchester and rented a property from Joseph Catchpole in the Holy Trinity district of that ancient town.* By this time John's father was well established as a coachman and victualler. John's sister Elizabeth was born in Colchester on 31 August 1790 and was baptized at the Church of the Holy Trinity.

In 1791 John's father met William Woods and they soon became good friends as they had a great deal in common. William owned the coaching firm of Woods and Co. and his coaches travelled between Sudbury, Hedingham and Braintree to Colchester and Chelmsford and from thence to London.

1795 was the turning point in John French senior's fortunes, when his Aunt Alice died. She had been the

* Land Tax Assessment of 1790

widow of the Sudbury baker, Anthony French. When the latter died, he left his money and property to his widow and then to his son Anthony. This was John's cousin and close friend Anthony who had sadly died in 1787. Thus with Alice's death and after the main bequest of the property having been made to Anthony Senior's brother Samuel, all Anthony and Alice's nephews and nieces received five pounds. John invested this money in William Woods' firm and thus the new firm of French and Woods was established.

His son John later set about increasing the number of coach trips from two to three from the Spread Eagle in Gracechurch Street and the Green Dragon in Bishopsgate which greatly helped the firm of French and Woods to become a success financially.[*]

In 1792, John Senior had moved to Chelmsford where he obtained the licence for the Ship Inn in the High Street. Shrewdly he had identified a gap in the market, namely that travellers from London would require somewhere convivial to eat and sleep at the end of their long coach journey. This new venture proved to be a great success.

Five more sisters joined John Junior in the family in Chelmsford, the last Louisa being born in 1803. John Junior inherited his father's love of horses and at about the age of thirteen he started to work as a coachman for his father's firm.

The Ship Inn was two doors down from the King's Head Inn whose proprietor was Gainsford Dixon. He was a widower, his wife having died in 1798. Gainsford had married Sarah Saunders on 31 October 1779 at Saint James Church in Piccadilly, and by 1787 he was the Landlord of the King's Head Inn in the High Street in

[*]   Boyds Directory for Chelmsford

Chelmsford. In this year he is mentioned in the *Chelmsford Chronicle*'s report of the Annual Three-day Flat Race Meeting.* This event was held on Galleywood Common and Gainsford had engaged a ladies hairdresser to provide a professional service as an entertainment for the ladies. This was a Mr Ward from Jermyn Street in Saint James London where Gainsford used to live before he moved to Essex. Mr Ward advertised himself as being honoured to accept all the ladies' commands and furthermore to do so 'with the strictest punctuality being equipped with all that was needed to compleat a Ladies hairstyle in the most elegant and newest fashions'.

When his wife died, Gainsford had to bring up his young daughter on his own and it is very likely that John Senior's wife Ann helped him as they were such near neighbours. Also John Senior and Gainsford were not only colleagues in the licensed trade but had also become close friends. Further they both acted as Trustees for each other, thus providing the surety for each other's Inns. Their friendship continued until Gainsford's death in 1802.

In his will, Gainsford left all his copyhold properties in Springfield Lane to Sarah with the proviso that if she died these properties were to pass to his brothers Charles and John or their heirs.

In these circumstances, it was inevitable that John Junior and Sarah Dixon would become friendly too and so on 23 February 1808 they were married at Saint Mary's Church in Chelmsford. All John's family attended the wedding including his Uncle George who was just establishing the thrice a day Coach and Wagon link between Malden and Chelmsford as part of his brother's overall business.

*   Chelmsford Chronicle July 1787

John and Sarah settled down to married life in Chelmsford. Their first child John Gainsford was born on 31 October 1809. His brother George followed him on 23 June 1811. The couple then had six daughters, namely Sarah, Ann, Elizabeth, Frances, Isabella and Ellen Louisa between 1813 and 1821. They then had three more sons, William Balls and Edward Dawson both of whom died as babies, and their last child Henry who was born on 30 December 1828.

By 1812, John was well established in running the coaching side of the business as a coachmaster while his father was in charge of The Ship Inn.

On 6 October of the same year, John was made a freeman of Colchester which not only enabled him to vote in elections in Chelmsford but also to take an active interest in the politics of the day and of his own home town in particular.*

In 1757, Pitt had introduced his Militia Bill in Parliament which was initiated to defend England from invasion This ordered that the militia be set up in all the various counties, as the regular militia was not getting sufficient recruits to fight in the current wars in Europe. As a result of this Act, each Parish established a kind of conscription by which all adult men were listed and ballots were made to choose those who would have to do military service. In 1816 John was listed and was selected for service.** However there is no evidence to show that he did anything more than a few days training. His brother in law William Murrell, however, was called up and became a Corporal in the Essex Militia.

John was also a very practical man and became very

*   Colchester Register of Freemen October 1812
** Local Militia List for Chelmsford Hamlet of Moulsham 1816

interested in improving the performance of the coaches, which plied between Chelmsford and London. He felt it was very important to increase their capacity for more travellers and in so doing increase the Company's profits. He was similar to the later William French in the fact that he quickly assimilated the newest engineering practices of the day. Thus in 1826, he launched his new Long Coach which had the awe-inspiring name of 'Patent Locomotive Carriage'. The name of French was emblazoned across both sides of the coach which could accommodate between twelve and eighteen passengers both inside and outside.

By the end of the eighteenth century the population of Chelmsford had increased significantly despite the bad harvest and freezing winter of 1799. Between 1815 and 1841 the numbers in fact had risen from 3,755 to 6,789. One of the main reasons for this was that Chelmsford had become a garrison town and with the advent of the Napoleonic Wars there had been a rapid build up of the regular Militia in the town. The Militia was quartered in barracks in the town and was in a state of readiness to either repel a French invasion or to serve abroad. However this fear of impending war did not in any way disrupt the life of the townspeople who carried on with life very much as usual.

This increase in population was also partly accounted for by the fact that fourteen miles of the River Chelmer had been opened for navigation with a system of sea locks and wharves in 1797. This resulted in coal being delivered more cheaply to the residents and also being supplied to the New Street Iron Foundry, which had been established in 1809 in response to the Industrial Revolution and employed a large number of workers. Thus the people were not only able to keep warm but there were many more jobs available.

As the population increased so did the need for affordable housing, which resulted in a great deal of house building and redevelopment. In 1795 Thomas Berney Bramston said, 'there was a rage for building.' Many of the older and dilapidated houses were knocked down and replaced with two storey properties, which were occupied by the middle classes. Others were merely modernized by such methods as refronting with brick or replacing the Georgian bow fronted windows with the latest plate glass ones. One of the areas of the town to be redeveloped was Springfield Lane, which was just round the corner from the Ship Inn and the offices of French and Woods and where Sarah already owned a number of properties. The owner of a number of old brick kilns in the lane had demolished them and had built sixteen low rent cheap homes in their place. These were rated at one pound and forty pence in the Land Tax Assessment of 1830.* Over the years John purchased most of these houses as an investment, from which he received a steady rent which supplemented the rents he received from the properties which Sarah had received from her father Gainsford in his will. They later became part of what was known as French Square. There were many other examples of this cheap and speculative housing going on at the same time all over the town.

With the birth of Henry in 1828 the family was now complete and John Junior and Sarah were happily contemplating a comfortable life. Their eldest son John Gainsford was doing very well at the Royal College of Veterinarians and George was working as coachman for the family firm.

However life is not always predictable and in John and

---

* Land Tax Assessment for Chelmsford 1830

Sarah's case it quickly became a nightmare. In April 1829 their son Edward died aged only twenty months, the most likely cause being consumption, which was to carry off so many of John's family.

In 1830, their daughter Sarah became apprenticed as a milliner to Mary Scrivener of 3 George Street just off Hanover Square in London. She was following in the footsteps of her sister Frances and more than likely went to London with her cousin, Ann Dean who was also a milliner. The two girls joined four other girls who were working there, but sadly Sarah died in November 1831 and was brought back to Chelmsford to be buried in the graveyard of Saint Mary's Church alongside her grandmother Ann who had died in 1822.

Then in the July of 1832 Frances also died. Meanwhile John himself died in September 1835 and George followed him in the December. The most probable cause was tuberculosis, the curse of the family.

John left a will, which was valued at Probate for two thousand pounds. In this, he left his share in French and Woods to his sons John Gainsford and George, together with the profits. He also left them his hearse, black coach, corn and harnesses.

He had also assured his life for one thousand pounds, which was to be divided between his four surviving daughters namely Ann, Elizabeth, Isabella and Ellen.

His wife Sarah was left all the houses in Springfield Lane and on her death they were to go to Henry. She was also left all his money, furniture, linen and plate.

Sarah was a strong and courageous woman as well as being very intelligent and soon after the death of her husband, she was back working as the Proprietor of French and Woods Coach Company in Baddow Lane where she carried on working until 1840.

She then bought the lovely big house called Sandon Place in Sandon, a little village outside Chelmsford. Here she and her daughters, who were teachers, opened a school. The house had four reception rooms downstairs, which were used as schoolrooms, as well as a kitchen. Upstairs there were six bedrooms for girls like her granddaughter Elizabeth who wanted to board. There was also a cottage in the grounds to accommodate their two servants whom they brought with them from Chelmsford. She and her three daughters Ann, Isabella and Ellen successfully ran Sandon Lodge as a Ladies School for a four years.

All went well until September 1845 when Isabella died of consumption and Ellen died also of the same disease in March 1851. Very much saddened and disheartened, Sarah sold Sandon Place and bought a small house in Widford on the Street where she lived with Ann. At this point in her life she merely described herself as a proprietor of lands and houses.

However she and Ann and her granddaughter Elizabeth Meadowcroft were back in Chelmsford by 1856 when they opened another school or seminary for eighteen children. Sarah stayed there until her death on 22 June 1859 of diarrhoea.

Three of John and Sarah's children married. Elizabeth being the first to do so, got married with Sarah's permission by licence on 7 April 1836 at Saint Runwold's Church in Colchester. As she was only twenty years old she was classified as a minor. Her bridegroom was Thomas Meadowcroft a good family friend who was also a chemist in Colchester. All the family attended the wedding and her grandfather was one of the witnesses along with her sister Ann. The couple had three children, Elizabeth born in June 1837, Thomas born in May 1838 and Mary who was born in July 1839. However Mary died from inflammation seven months later and Elizabeth never really got over this. Eventually her husband sent her to stay with her mother at Sandon in a vain effort to help her to get over her depression but she died of decline there in February 1841.

Elizabeth's daughter Elizabeth lived with her father after the death of her grandmother Sarah and went to the School for Girls in Crouch Street in Colchester where she was a very good pupil. However, by 1862 she had taken over her grandmother's school for girls at 7 Western Terrace Moulsham. A 17-year-old pupil teacher Jessie Clark assisted her.

In 1840 a young Professor of Music, James Dace moved to Chelmsford. In 1843,* he invited the nobility and the gentry together with the ordinary inhabitants of Chelmsford to attend his Evening Concert on 22 May. This was being held at the Mechanics' Institute and the main reason for this free concert was to attract new pupils from the town and outlying villages to attend his school of music. The programme was advertised as consisting of a choice selection of music from the works of Mozart, Thalberg, Labitzky, Davaux and many others. At this time James was the organist at All Saints Church in Maldon.

The *Chelmsford Chronicle* in its report of the event said that the concert was very poorly attended despite being free. It went on to describe how well James played both the piano and organ. He got an ovation for his interpretation of the quadrille Les Plaisirs de L'Industrie** which he played with great ability and mastery. He was very ably assisted by a small orchestra consisting of Messrs

*   Announcement Chelmsford Chronicle 22 May 1843
**   Report of the event in the Chelmsford Chronicle May 1843

W. and R. Waring, Messrs C., W., and J. Fuller, Mr Potter and Mr Orrell who played the violins, a cello and a contra bass respectively. However the other member of the Orchestra, Mr Dennis laboured under great difficulties to play his flute. The *Chelmsford Chronicle* also praised the Professor's masterly style and ability to conduct and hoped that a second concert would attract a bigger audience.

James continued to be the organist at Maldon until 1848 and then moved to Colchester when he again advertised in the *Chronicle* that he would visit his Chelmsford pupils every Wednesday and Thursday as well as visiting his other pupils in Writtle, Maldon and Witham on Thursday. He left Essex for a couple of years when he went to live in Leamington Spa but this was not a success and so by 1851 he was back again in Chelmsford and living at 5 Weston Terrace. He also rented a warehouse in 1859 at 1 Institute Terrace, New London Road where he stored the pianos and harmoniums he had for sale at his shop in the town. In 1862 he opened another store at The Grove, Stratford as well as starting a repair business at his second Chelmsford store at 145 High Road. In the next four years he opened branches at Colchester and Romford as well.

One wonders whether Elizabeth met James as her music teacher or whether they met for the first time when they were near neighbours but suffice it to say that they became friendly and on 9 November 1863 they got married at Saint John's Church Moulsham. Her father Thomas who had moved from Colchester to Wolverhampton gave Elizabeth away. After the wedding, the couple continued to live in Chelmsford at New Bridge Street.

However in 1866, they moved to 21 High Street Colchester, which was just opposite Saint Runwold's

Parish Church. The couple went on to have four children, Arthur Wellington, Ernest Waring, Eva and Laura. James died on 3 September 1896 and Elizabeth died on 15 October of the same year. They were both buried with two of their children who had died earlier in Colchester cemetery.

James Dace left a Will and the estate was valued at Probate at £3,724 14s 10d. He left all his furniture and other household effects to his two daughters Eva and Laura and he also left them a legacy of five hundred and fifty pounds free of legacy duty. He left five hundred pounds to his son Ernest. Finally he left the residue of his personal estate to his elder son Arthur. The company of James Dace and Son is still trading in Chelmsford today.

John and Sarah's youngest surviving son was Henry. He went to live with John Gainsford after the latter's marriage and there he took an apprenticeship with a Chelmsford butcher where he stayed until he had finished his training. When John Gainsford went to Maldon, Henry moved to London to work and his first job was at a butcher's shop in Kingsland Road, Shoreditch, London.

On 11 September 1848, he married Mary Ann Pritchard of Bromley, Kent at Saint Leonard's Church in Shoreditch. She was the daughter of the late William Pritchard and his widow Matilda. Soon after the marriage, Henry moved to Cheshunt Street in Cheshunt, Hertfordshire. Here he and Mary Ann had their three daughters, Catherine Matilda, Annie Sarah and Lizzie Jane in 1849, 1856 and 1859 respectively.

After the death of his mother, Henry inherited the houses in Springfield Road but he most probably sold these to his brother John Gainsford. This financial arrangement not only enabled Henry to buy his first shop but also entitled John to vote in the Chelmsford election as he held the copyhold of these Springfield Lane properties.*

The shop was the same one in Kingsland Road Shoreditch where Henry had previously worked, which had just come up for sale. However it was not very long before he bought a better shop in Tottenham with his inheritance from his Aunt Isabella. This was very near to John Gainsford's home at Downhills Farm. Later he inherited a further fifty pounds from his Aunt Rebecca in 1875 and these inheritances certainly helped the family financially. Henry lived in Tottenham until his death from Cancer on 24 June 1890. His widow and his eldest daughter Catherine who was also a widow took over the running of the shop.

Henry's will was valued at £570 12s 6d and he left his wife four hundred pounds from a Life Insurance Policy which he had taken out with the Prudential Life Society of Holborn. He left his stock book, silver, plate and furniture to Catherine together with all the old family paintings and the Dace piano.

Finally this chapter would not be complete without the poem which Sarah wrote in her Bible in 1823.

One little ray of light O Lord
I humbly ask of thee
To guide me thro' thy written word
That I thy will may see.

Thy Holy Spirit's aid impart
To cheer me on my way
And give my Lord a grateful heart
To adore thee and obey.

*   1874 Chelmsford Register of Electors

CHAPTER 7

John French
1760–1840

This chapter starts in the delightful little town of Sudbury in Suffolk. Here the old houses and the rural surroundings gave it an idyllic feel. The River Stour bordered the town to the north and west, and also provided it with a good source of communication. The establishment of the freemen's lands further blessed the town as these comprised of more than forty acres of meadowland where the freemen were able to graze their cattle, which gave them a better diet, and if they chose to give up this right they got an increased monetary income. However despite what to the outsider in the eighteenth century might believe, this was not the sleepy hollow away from the main stream of life that it seemed.

The town was a Borough with its own Charter, which ensured that the Council and the freemen governed it. This entitled any man to become a freeman either by right of heredity, or if he had been apprenticed for seven years in the town. This right was greatly prized and the Minutes in the Court Books of the Sudbury Borough Court were far from dull, with many lively debates. However Sudbury and the Council also had its fair share of disgraceful Members of Parliament, appalling mayors and restive and even turbulent people.

On the positive side, the town had established a very progressive Sunday School system by the mid eighteenth century which enabled many of its young girls and boys to learn to read and write in an elementary fashion.

The town also had its full complement of shops, inns and ancillary jobs. After agriculture the main occupation in the town had been that of weaving but between 1700 and 1780 this had suffered a severe decline. Although by 1780 weaving overall was also a declining industry in England.

John French was baptized on 31 March 1760 at Saint Peter's Church in the town. This John was the most dynamic of the French family and his intelligence and robust energy was a most significant factor in the start of the change in both the French family's financial and social position.

John was the third child born to John French a weaver and his wife Mary late Keble. The first two of their children were girls, the first being Mary who was born on 2 February 1754 and who died on 16 November of the same year. Her sister Alice was born on 17 of January 1758 and John followed two years later. John and Mary then had five more sons, James, Samuel, Anthony, Thomas and George as well as two other daughters Mary and Sarah.

John was a very bright boy and attended the Sunday School where he learned the rudiments of reading and writing from his weekly study of the bible. When he was eleven, the family became embroiled in the political riot of 1771 for which his father was the lighted fuse. Shortly after this John became a weaver and worked alongside his father until the latter's death in November 1780. In August 1781, John was admitted to the Freedom of the town of Sudbury as a weaver as being the son of John, a weaver, who was now deceased as well as having been born in the borough.

About this time, John met and married Ann, the daughter of Henry Ginn a bricklayer in the town and his wife Rachel. Henry like John was also a Freeman of the Borough and in 1792 was sworn in as a Sergeant at Mace when he also supported the Constitution in that year.

The young couple were married at Saint Peter's Church in the town by Banns on 1 April 1782. John was supported at the service by both his cousin Anthony and his very good friend Elias Cleare a lace maker.

John and Ann very quickly started a family with the arrival of their first born Ann on 25 March 1783. She was followed by Sarah on 25 October 1784 and John on 26 November 1786.

Very sadly their daughter Sarah died on 15 September 1787 most probably of the 'putrid fever' which was raging in the town and surrounding countryside. This naturally caused John and Ann great sadness and John decided to rethink his future prospects. He pondered over the possible direction his life should take and which would hopefully change it for the better. By late 1786, he had started working as a victualler. This initially had been undertaken to help his uncle Samuel and his cousin Anthony get the supplies for their businesses. Both of them were bakers in the town, although Samuel had in the early 1760s leased the George Inn there. John began trading between Sudbury and Colchester and the couple decided to move to the latter town. They thought it would be more convenient for John's new work and also give them the change of scene they both needed. They lived for a while in the All Saints area of the town in a property owned by Joseph Catchpole.

John and his cousin Anthony remained very close and when the latter was to get married to Sarah Ginn of Dedham, John accompanied him to obtain a marriage licence in March 1786. He gave his employment as victualler and not weaver. In 1790 the Poll Book of that year officially described him as a coachman of Colchester. The last time he voted in Sudbury was in the Parliamentary Election of 1790 when he voted for William Smith and John Pardoe the younger.

After their son John was born, the couple had two more daughters, Hannah who was born in Sudbury on 16 June 1788 and Elizabeth who was baptized on 31 August 1790 at the Holy Trinity Church in Colchester.

However the main turning point in John's life came on 28 June 1795 when his Aunt Alice the mother of his cousin Anthony died in Sudbury.* In her husband's Will his property and money was to pass to her son Anthony the younger who had himself died on 3 October 1787. However his father had made provision for this eventuality and stated that if this did happen, his property was to be passed to his brother Samuel after each of his and Alice's nephew and nieces had inherited five pounds. This was a good sum of money and changed John's fortune and circumstances forever.

While John was working as a coachman and victualler, he had made the acquaintance of William Woods who owned his own coaching firm of William Woods and Co in Chelmsford. His coaches plied their trade between London and Sudbury and they stopped on the way in Chelmsford. On receiving his legacy, John invested it in this firm.

Thus in 1792, John and Ann decided to move south again to Chelmsford as this was a strategic place on the coach route to London. Rebecca was their first child to be baptized from their new home. This event took place

* Will of Anthony French 1780

at Saint Mary' Church on 10 June in that year. She was
followed by Maria in 1796, Isabella in 1798 and finally
by Louisa in 1803. In those unenlightened times, John
and Ann were totally unlike many of their peers insofar
as their treatment of their daughter Maria was concerned.
She had been born with some form of mental deficiency
and instead of abandoning her, they cared for her tenderly
at home as did her sisters when their parents died. In fact
John left Maria the bulk of his money in his will and
she lived with the family and assisted in as far as she was
able in the running of their inn until she was too ill to
stay at home.

After John received his inheritance of five pounds he
not only joined William Woods as co-owner of the
Coaching Firm but had also taken over the licence in
1792 of the Ship Inn, which he bought in 1806.

He also became a Freeman of Colchester and continued
to be very active in the politics of the day. In 1796, he
was one of the only two permitted voters in Chelmsford
who voted in the Colchester Poll.* His occupation was
given as a victualler and the other voter was the
schoolmaster William Alexander. Subsequently he always
voted in his capacity as an innkeeper in an ever increasing
list for Chelmsford and never missed this privilege until
his death.

However his main preoccupation over the next few
years was the consolidation of his business and financial
affairs.

Until 1806, John and the family were living in the Ship
Inn where he was the Licensee.** However in 1806,***

---

*   Colchester Poll Book
**   Chelmsford Registered Persons licensed to Inn in the town
*** Bundle of documents in ERO numbers D/D Yr

he purchased the Old Ship Inn, which comprised of the inn he lived in and another inn, the Ipswich Arms next door. He bought this property from James Parker a chinaman and his wife Mary who was the sister of the previous owner of the Ship, Sarah Lough, a baker. She herself had originally bought the Ship and the Ipswich Arms next door. The latter was also the Judges' Lodgings for the town when the justices came to town. This had been occupied before John French bought it by The Chelmsford Machine, which had been run by Daniel Baker and John Woods, William's father. John used it for his Chelmsford firm of French and Woods.

John and the family continued to live in the Ship Inn. This had been built sometime before 1756 when it had been sold to John Reid who had bought it from its previous owner John Ward, a merchant from London who went bankrupt. John Ward's son Ralph, a merchant who was trading in Riga, together with John Ward's attorney Thomas Spencer of London agreed to the sale on condition that £400 together with the interest should be paid to John Ward's estate.

The inn was later purchased by Ann Goodwin, the widow of John Goodwin a coachmaster of Chelmsford, who sold it on to Daniel Baker an innkeeper. He in turn sold it to Sarah Lough who died in 1806. In her will of that year, Sarah left the inn to her only sister, Mary the wife of James Parker, who sold it to John French for sixty pounds. The property consisted of a messuage, three stables, and three coach houses together with the haylofts, land, gardens and water.

It was also in this year that the High Sheriff of Essex pointed out the inadequacy of the Ipswich Arms as a lodging place for the Judges, as the property had been allowed to deteriorate badly and was even in danger of falling down. As a result the Judges were moved to the more opulent surroundings of Mr Oxley Parker's building in the High Street. John French then modernized the old Ship Inn and the Ipswich Arms to suit his customers. In fact it became so comfortable that the London passengers who alighted from the French and Woods Coaches really enjoyed their stay in the town.

In 1818*, John bought twelve acres of land, four acres of woodland, five more coach houses and two gardens both in Chelmsford and Stow Maries a small country village. He bought this with William Woods and his old friend Charles Parker of Springfield. William was by this time the innkeeper of the Silent Woman at Ingatestone. On his move he had sold John his share in the Ship for five shillings in the same year. So now John was the owner of the Ship and the co-proprietor of the Coaching Firm.

In 1836**, William Woods having died, his son Henry offered John his father's share in the business for one thousand pounds. However John replied by letter to decline this offer. The next year, after the death of his son John Junior and as he was by then a very old man John himself entered into an agreement to re lease the properties in 1837.*** He did this in conjunction with William Woods' three sons, Henry who was an innkeeper in Aldersgate Street in the City of London, John who was a coal merchant and lived in Brompton and Frederick who was a surveyor of Ingatestone. John's grandson John Gainsford made up the fourth party to the agreement.

From all this acquisition of property, we can deduce

---

*   Bundle of documents in ERO D/D Yr 23–42
**   As above
***   As above

that John had not only done very well for himself
financially but he also had acquired a very different status
from that which he had held as a weaver in Sudbury. He
had most certainly used his intelligence and drive to
greatly improve the business and also had used the
monetary rewards this brought to purchase property,
which were all the hallmarks of the middle classes.

To show his social importance it is interesting to see
his contribution to the great fire that broke out in the
middle of the night on Saturday 19 March in the dining
room at Brettons on Poultry Hill on the High Street.*
This was a two-storey property with an attic and was
situated at the end of a small row of mean houses. It was
also very close to some timber framed warehouses, coach
houses and stables in Back Street. All in all it was a
disastrous place for such a fire to start as most of the
buildings were wooden and would burn very easily.

Mrs Smith the owner of Brettons carried out her
millinery business there. At the time of the fire there were
six adults and a child who were fast asleep upstairs in
this house. Luckily a servant at the chemist shop next
door was woken up by the noise of the fire crackling as
well as the flickering lights, which lit up his attic bedroom.
He raised the alarm and his employer Mrs Peck ran out
of the house and started banging on all the doors of the
nearby houses to warn them about the fire. Poor Mrs
Smith at Brettons was woken up too late to escape as
the fire had already spread throughout all the downstairs
rooms of her home. Thus both she and all the others
were trapped. The book entitled 'Narrative of the late
Deplorable Fire' and costing a shilling, later was to tell
of this terrible night and described how Mrs Smith being

*   Narrative of the Late Deplorable Fire at Chelmsford

trapped by the fire appeared at her bedroom window with the child and called out for help. At the same time, two seamstresses at another window also shouted out hysterically for assistance. The bystanders who had gathered on the path below looked up with horror and a few men led by the ironmonger Mr Wood hurried off to try and find a ladder from one of the yards behind the house. Before they could find one, the two young seamstresses had jumped out of the window to the ground thirty feet below. Mercifully they were not killed and although they were injured they both recovered. Eventually the men found a ladder and Mr Sorrel, a gardener, was able to rescue the servant girl who had crawled out of another window and was clinging to the parapet.

Two more servant girls came to their window but were too frightened to climb out. Meanwhile Henry Guy climbed up the ladder again and brought down the child whom Mrs Smith was holding. By this time the fire had got a real hold and had surrounded the ladder. When Henry got to the ground, Robert Guy's servant went up and dragged Mrs Smith out of the window. However she was a very large and heavy woman and was not only terrified but was also naked so he had nothing to grab a hold of. He tried to support her as he got her out but she fell to the ground below at the very moment the upstairs of the house collapsed in a ball of flames.

All the other occupants of the adjoining little houses had escaped into the street and some of them had even managed to salvage a few bits and pieces before they made their escape. However by this time the fire was out of control and racing up the High Street placing the town in terrible danger.

The fire engines quickly arrived manned by the Loyal

Chelmsford Volunteers. They decided that it was best to use the water from the conduit to damp down the shopfronts and the shutters of the houses in the High Street while the fire engine concentrated its jet on the fronts of the buildings in Back Street which was behind Brettons. However they all believed that the whole town's existence was on a knife-edge as a whole row of buildings next to Brettons was by this time completely demolished by the fire. As the fire engine got to work on one side of the High Street over a hundred men formed a human chain and passed along buckets of water from the ditch at the bottom of Robert Kelham's garden to damp down the house frontages on the High Street.

In the end Chelmsford was saved but the little row of houses behind Brettons and eight houses in the High Street were very badly damaged.

Far worse than this was the death of Mrs Smith and the two frightened servant girls who were unable to climb out of their window. The two coffins of these girls, Miss Woolmar and Miss Eve, who had so dreadfully perished were removed to the Ship Inn at the far end of the High Street, owned by John French. This was done for safety and to accommodate the solemn procession to the Church for the funerals.*

This procession passed in silence and the whole town turned out to mourn the loss of the two girls. About an hour before this funeral, Mrs Smith died peacefully having lingered in great torment for seven days. She never knew about the death of her two servants.

The people who had lost their homes were accommodated in the House of Correction and The Sun Fire Assurance agents Meggy and Chalk formally thanked

---

*   The late Deplorable Fire at Chelmsford

all those who had helped to save their offices. Mrs Peck was also very delighted when the Phoenix Insurance Company met her claim very speedily. The whole town raised a subscription towards the relief of the sufferers, which raised the princely total of £629 of which John French donated two guineas.*

The final example of John French's improved financial and social position can be seen in the part that he played in the Coronation celebrations for George the Fourth. George when he had been Prince Regent had revived the annual sponsorship of the Annual One Hundred Guineas Race at Galleywood, which had really greatly improved his popularity in Chelmsford. As a result the prominent men of the town decided to have a really spectacular Gala celebration for his Coronation. The public rejoicing began with the church bells ringing out at midnight and the following morning the townspeople were woken by the sound of four guns being discharged. This was the signal for the local dignitaries to parade through the town all singing the National Anthem. Meanwhile tables were set out in front of the Shire Hall in Conduit Square and at one o'clock the meal for two thousand respectable people both rich and poor from the town began. After the blessing, they feasted off a really sumptuous meal of beef and fat ox, bread and plum pudding and as they finished the meat, the band played 'Oh the Roast Beef of Old England'.** When the ordinary folk had been fed there was a further procession through the town with flags flying and 'God save the King' being sung lustily.

At four o'clock a hundred gentlemen from the town, including I am sure John French and his son, had their

---

*   Alphabetical list of the subscribers to the relief of the Sufferers
**   Chelmsford Chronicle Friday July 20th 1821

dinner in the County Room of the Shire Hall. After the speeches the company went home being highly delighted with the conviviality of the occasion. In the evening there was a splendid firework display which passed off in a perfect manner.

This was not the only illumination that night, for all the buildings from the humblest tenement to the grandest house and shop were lit up with candles or the new gaslights. The Shire Hall and the Gaol together with the other public buildings were tastefully lit* and down the High Street the shop holders and innkeepers put displays in their windows and vied with each other to produce the best display. John French certainly played his part in this and his display drew the notice of the people. In the Coach House Office** window was a realistic seventy-four-gun man-of-war. This was not only a perfect model but also had the correct colours displayed and all the right coloured lamps on the rigging. The ship was placed on a moss bed to display it to its greatest advantage.

There were many busts displayed in other windows, mostly of the new King, and Mr Guy had Fame descending with the Crown.

The whole event was paid for by public subscription which raised the princely sum of £255 2s 6d.

John and Ann's eldest daughter was baptized at Saint Peter's Church on 25 March 1783. She went with the family to Essex to live where she met and married the son of her father's friend Charles Murrell. This was William Bartwell Murrell who had served as a Corporal in the second troop of the Essex Yeomanry, having been

*   Chelmsford Chronicle Friday July 20th 1821
**   As above

selected from the Muster Roll of 1799.* He had been born in 1782, being the son of Charles and Elizabeth of Springfield. Charles like John French was also a Licensee of an inn, the Three Cups, and they became very good friends. The young couple were married at Saint Mary's Church by Licence on 21 May 1805. Both Ann's father and brother together with the latter's young lady friend Sarah Dixon signed the register. After their marriage, William and Ann ran the Three Cups Inn at Springfield. William was the licensee and after his death Ann took over the licence and the running of the Inn. She must have not only been a splendid manager but also a very kind person as these attributes were rewarded in her mother in law's Will of 1826. In this, Elizabeth left Ann her antique gold watch, which had been in the Murrell family for many years and which she had herself inherited from the family. On the death of her husband she had made it into a mourning watch in his memory. She left her estate to her three sons but she specifically stated that Ann was not only to make all the funeral arrangements but also was to take over the complete management of her home and moreover to take possession of her keys. This was very significant as it meant that Ann had full control of the household.

Ann and William had three children, William Bartwell who was born on 3 November 1810, Ann who was born on Christmas Day 1805 and Sarah on 25 February 1813. Each of these children were left £20 10s 2d in Ann's father's Will.

When the two eldest children grew up they assisted their mother in the day to day running of the inn. William

*   Muster Roll of the persons enrolled and serving in the second troop of Essex Gentlemen and Yeomanry

used his spare time to play a great deal of cricket for the team in Springfield and in fact in September 1841, he purchased his own new cricket field. At the opening of this new ground, he made a useful innings of ten runs against the opposing side from Ingatestone. The match was watched by a thousand spectators who greatly commended the playing of Murrell.*

Sarah married the farmer and dealer Robert Howard on 5 May 1834. He lived at Chignall Saint James and later the couple and their burgeoning family moved to Great Baddow.

Her sister Ann and her brother William took over the running of the Three Cups on the death of their mother on 21 July 1856.

On her death Ann left her three children sixty pounds for their immediate use. However a year or so before her death Ann had sold the Three Cups to Mr Praed Wood for £1,600 at auction with the proviso that she should continue to live and work in the Inn during her lifetime. In her will she stated that she had ensured that her children had the first option to buy the inn back at her death at this same price plus the auction dues, which they in fact did.

Her daughter Ann never married and continued to live and work at the inn with her brother.

William married Mary Ann Shipcott on 11 June 1861 at Saint John of Hackney Church and the three continued to run the Three Cups together until William and Ann's deaths in 1881. William and Mary had three sons William Augustus, Charles Baker and Patrick Arthur.

John and Ann's second daughter was Hannah and she was born on 16 June 1788 and was baptized on 29 July

* Chelmsford Chronicle 3 September 1841

1796 at Saint Peter's Church in Sudbury. Her Grandmother had died in March of that year and the family would have no doubt returned to Sudbury for the Funeral. It is also very likely that the Priest had remarked that Hannah had never been baptized as the family had been on the move at the time of her birth. So they agreed to return in the summer for the christening and no doubt they were pleased to have this performed in the town where she had been born.

Hannah also married a friend of the family who was in fact more her brother's friend. His name was James Dean who was a Bank Clerk. The couple married on 3 October 1809 at the parish church in Chelmsford like Hannah's sister before her. James was five years older than Hannah, being 33 when he answered the Militia Muster in 1816. The couple had three children, James who was born in January 1811, John French who was born and died in 1813 in Chelmsford and Ann who was born in December 1823. By this time the family had moved from Chelmsford to Ingatestone, where James was employed as the Clerk to the Estate Manager, Mr Coverdale of Ingatestone Hall. Soon after this James died and Hannah brought up the children alone.

Her son James married Maria Watson on 23 December 1839 at Saint Leonard's Church Shoreditch and the couple moved back to Springfield where James worked in the Gaol. They had two children, Maria Ann in 1840 and James in April 1843. Maria herself died seven months later in the November. James had started his working life as a Turnkey at the Chelmsford Gaol where he had a somewhat chequered career. In April 1837 he was recommended for dismissal for negligence as he had allowed a prisoner to escape. However after making a petition to the Governor he got his job back and instead of dismissal he paid ten pounds towards the cost of getting the prisoner back. He then worked very hard and became the Deputy Governor. He had a staff of three warders under him together with two watchmen and a turnkey. James must have continued to enjoy a drink as he was subsequently dismissed for being drunk in 1853. During this time his son James was being educated at Greenbury School in Writtle* and his daughter Maria Ann was being looked after by her grandparents Edward and Sarah Watson in their home in Randolph Terrace Springfield. Maria Ann later took an apprenticeship to train as a milliner like her two cousins Sarah and Frances before her.

James then moved back into Chelmsford and started work as a Land Surveyor and in 1858 he remarried. He and his new wife Sophie moved to live in the Springfield Road where James became a solicitor's clerk. Sophie died in 1869 and as James felt unable to live alone, he went to live with his married sister Ann. She was living in Holly Cottage in Hampstead with her husband Richard Little, a clerk in a publishing office. James himself died in Highgate Infirmary of a stroke on 4 April 1872.

Meanwhile their mother Hannah who, although she had inherited £250 2s 8d from her father in 1840, was finding life a struggle, especially financially.

After the death of her father Hannah had found work in Chelmsford with Jacob Farrow who had the shop on the High Street between the house where John Gainsford and his wife Sarah lived and the Ship where her sisters were. Farrow was the town plumber. Hannah eventually left Chelmsford in the mid forties and moved to Colchester where she became the housekeeper for Robert Tabrum a

*   1851 Census

grocer in East Street. She continued to work there until she was well into her seventies.

However she lived out the last years of her life very happily with her daughter Ann and died at her home at the age of eighty-five on 22 February 1874. Ann and Richard had moved from Hampstead by then and were living at 5 Victoria Terraces, 1 Avenue Road, Tottenham. On Hannah's death, she left her Gas shares to her son James and all her furniture to Ann. She left her capital of three hundred pounds to be divided between both of them in equal parts.

Louisa was the third daughter of John and Ann to get married. She was born on 22 February 1803 and like her sister was baptized at Saint Mary's Church Chelmsford. She married William Webb on 22 October 1828 in Brighton. The couple got married by Licence on which William gave his address as Brighthelmston, the name for Brighton in Victorian times and he did not give his occupation. Louisa gave her address as the same as William's. At the time William was, in fact a waiter and I rather think Louisa was in the same line of work. They both said they were twenty-one. The couple had three sons very quickly. In 1829 William John was born and George followed him in 1832. Frederick Thomas was the third son and he was born in 1836. After these three boys William and Louisa had their last child, a little girl. For a while they could not decide on a name as she was registered without a name but eventually they had her baptized Maria Louisa in 1838.

William was employed as a servant in 1829 but was a waiter again by 1832. He continued in this job until he was forty-five years old.

In 1851 Louisa died of tuberculosis which was the scourge of the French family. She was only 48 years old.

By this time her son William was a plumber and painter while his brother Frederick was a white smith.

After Louisa's death, her daughter Maria Louisa Webb went to live with her aunts in Chelmsford. They loved having her with them and greatly cared for her and she for them. While she was living in Essex she met and married Joseph Yell, a farmer from Great Baddow. The ceremony took place in London at Saint Botolph's Parish Church in Bishopsgate. Her aunts attended the wedding and Isabella signed the register. Joseph had inherited his farm Great Graces from his father. This was a quite a large concern as he employed seven men and five boys to help cultivate the land.

Joseph and Maria lived and worked on the farm where they had three boys, Joseph, born in 1864, Frank born in 1871 and Charles born in 1872. Joseph and Charles were still farming Great Graces in 1922. Their mother Maria Louisa died on 6 February 1915 at home at the farm. She was seventy-six years old and was buried at Little Baddow Church.

John and Ann's other three daughters Rebecca, Isabella and Maria never married. Rebecca had been baptized on 20 June 1792, Maria on 17 April 1796 and Isabella on 21 May 1798. All three baptisms took place at Saint Mary's Chelmsford.

After John's death in 1840 the three sisters all remained at the Ship where they had been helping their father for many years. In 1843, John Gainsford sold his fifth share in the Ship to his two aunts and in 1849 James Parker and the three other shareholders followed suit and sold their shares to Rebecca and Isabella. Thus the two sisters became the joint-owners and inn keepers of the

Ship Inn.* They both continued to care for Maria as well as allowing her to help in the work of the inn as much as she was able. For the next twenty years life continued in a very smooth manner.

In 1851 Maria Louisa came to live with them on the death of her mother. She settled in very happily and in no way altered their contented pattern of life.

However in early 1865, Isabella became ill and she died six months later of cancer, which was an enormous blow to Rebecca. Also by this time Maria was becoming a greater burden to Rebecca, as she was now on her own. Maria then had a stroke and Rebecca placed her in the care of the Essex Lunatic Asylum in South Weald where she died at the end of 1865.

This again hit Rebecca badly and in 1869 she felt obliged to rent out one of the stables as the large amount of stabling was getting a bit too much for her. She made an agreement with Henry Crozier the county beer retailer whom she knew through the inn, whereby he took over the main stable and loft at the Ship together with the yard. Soon after this, Rebecca who as well as being alone was also feeling the effects of her advancing years decided to move to a house in Springfield Terrace. Maria's son Joseph went and stayed with her quite often and they became firm friends. However in 1874, Maria invited her to live with her family at Great Graces. Rebecca was pleased to accept as not only was she eighty-four years old but also she herself was suffering with the early stages of cancer. Rebecca died in October 1875 with little Joseph beside her at Great Graces. The announcement in the *Chelmsford Chronicle* stated she was the last surviving daughter of John French of Chelmsford.

*   1841-1861 Census and Boyds Directory for Chelmsford

Both Isabella and Rebecca left very comprehensive wills. The former left six thousand pounds. In it, she left all the income, rents and dues from her personal estate to her sisters for their lifetime. She then left Maria Louisa her shares in the Chelsea Water Works. She also made a bequest of nineteen guineas to her goddaughter Isabella Howard and left Ann Murrell ten pounds. After all these legacies were paid, her personal estate was then to be sold. The proceeds were then to be divided equally between all her nephews and nieces, namely Maria Louisa, William Bartwell Murrell and his sister Ann and Sarah Howard, John Gainsford and Henry French, Maria Ann Little and the three Webb boys.

Rebecca in her will left her shares in the Chelmsford Gas and Water Companies to Maria Louisa. She then left legacies of three hundred pounds to William Bartwell Murrell and fifty pounds to his sister Ann and also to Elizabeth Dace her goddaughter. She left the eight children of her late sister Sarah five pounds each and finally she left Henry French, Ann Little and the three Webb boys fifty pounds. In 1874, George Webb had emigrated to Melbourne in Australia and he had to be in touch with the lawyer within a year to inherit his share. Finally after all these pecuniary legacies had been paid the Ship was to be sold either at auction or privately and the proceeds were to go to Maria Louisa. The property by this time consisted of the Ship itself, the house and the coach office and shop as well as the stables, sheds, warehouse, chaise house and the truckshed. These were all constructed of brick and tile. The sale went through and the Ship was subsequently sold to William Pascall in 1876.*

Both these Wills show the middle class position that

---

*   Document for the Sale of the Ship

the two sisters held as well as showing as in the case of
Maisie who lived years later how much family meant to
them.

John's wife Ann had died at the age of sixty-one on
14 February 1822 and was buried in the graveyard of
Saint Mary's Church in the family grave. She joined her
two daughters, Elizabeth who died in August 1807 and
Mary Ann who died as an infant. Finally on 12 May 1840
John himself. He was of the ripe old age of eighty, which
was indeed a great age in that era. He too was buried in
the family grave.*

The two obituaries in the *Chelmsford Chronicle* and
The Times stated that John died at the advanced age of
80 and had been the much respected coach proprietor of
the firm of Woods and French. The former stated that
he was for many years the proprietor of the old
Chelmsford coaches.** He was also the longest serving
licensee in the town of Chelmsford, having held the licence
for the Ship from 1792 until 1839.

John left a very long and complicated Will, which is
in fact written on a scroll of parchment and makes
fascinating reading.*** It comprised of six pages, which
were mainly concerned with the establishment of Trusts
in numerous hypothetical circumstances.

In essence, he gave the freehold messuage at the sign
of the Ship to his executors, his two friends Thomas
Moss, plasterer, of Chelmsford and George Augustus
George of Great Baddow and his daughter Rebecca. This
was to be used for the care of Maria a lunatic for her
lifetime. If Rebecca and Isabella remained unmarried they

---

*   The grave is no longer there as most of the graves have been removed
**   In the papers of the day
*** The Will is lodged at the Essex Record Office

were to live at the Ship and carry on the business. Further they were to ensure that Maria had eight pounds a year for her keep and that she was to be properly clothed. If they married they could lease the Ship with the permission of the other trustees. If however they sold the Ship they were to give three hundred pounds to Maria for her keep and three hundred pounds to Hannah and Louisa and if they were dead to their named offspring. He then gave all his personal estate and effects to both Isabella and Rebecca. The Will was dated 8 April 1840.

The other main financial provisions that John made were that he left Ann's three children £20 2s 7d each. He then left Hannah £200 10s 8d and Louisa £95 9s. As well as leaving Rebecca and Isabella the Ship, he also left them £300 11s 8d apiece. In all John left six hundred pounds, which is considerably more than the five pounds he inherited in 1795.*

---

*   Death Duties Register PRO 1840

CHAPTER 8

John French
1733–1780

John French was baptized on 2 February 1733 at Saint
Peter's Church in Sudbury. He was the third son of
Mayhew French and his wife Mary.

His eldest brother Mayhew had been baptized on 10
September 1727 in Little Waldingfield Church and his
other brother Anthony was baptized on 9 December 1730
in Saint Peter's in Sudbury.

In 1747 John was a pupil teacher at the Charity
School in Sudbury where he had received his education
each Sunday. Every child in the town was expected
to attend such a school except in exceptional
circumstances such as sickness. When he was later
dismissed from his position as a teacher at the school
with the consent of the Governors he stated that with
the agreement of his parents and to please God he was
returning ten shillings from the fifty pounds
which he had received from them to be used for the
upkeep of the school. He also thanked them* for his
education and for his religious life. He was moreover
able to write beautifully.

It is very likely that the young French boys made the
acquaintance of Sudbury's famous son Thomas
Gainsborough at the Sunday School. In the early 1740s

---

* Document at the Bury Branch of the Suffolk record office GB 532/2

Gainsborough gave a black chalk stump and white chalk picture to their cousin Richard French.* The picture was of a Mountain Landscape with Classical Buildings, a Shepherd and some Sheep. It was sold by the French family and eventually was bought by the National Gallery of Victoria, where it has remained in the vaults. I have however got a photograph of this picture.

John married Mary Keble at Saint Peter's Church on 8 May 1753 when they both were twenty years of age. John was a weaver in the town.

Perhaps John's greatest claim to fame was that he was one of the three catalysts which started the 1771 riot in the town.

In November 1771,** the *Ipswich Journal* informed its readers that they had been credibly informed that there was a great riot in Sudbury when the Corporation had assembled in the Town Hall. At noon the corporate body had been dissolved but they were then forcibly detained in the Town Hall until nine o'clock at night. Further they were denied access to their friends as well as to sustenance. When night came the populace put out their lights and repeatedly threatened their lives with stones and other more mischievous implements. Owing to the imminent danger the Corporation felt they were in, they were forced to comply with the terms that the populace had imposed on them. This preserved their lives and gave them their liberty. In the next edition of the *Journal* the paper remarked that as a consequence of the riot at Sudbury (mentioned in the last paper) a party of dragoons from Colchester marched in to the town to assist the civil magistrates preserve the peace.

---

*   Provenance of the painting from the National Gallery of Victoria
**   Ipswich column of the Ipswich Journal November 1771

On 31 January the paper gave notice that a Rule was made absolute in the Court of the King's Bench, for an Information against the principal persons concerned in the riot at Sudbury on 29 October the last. They also wrote that they had heard from Sudbury that the Corporation had held a court there at which they filled up three vacancies in the body of capital burgesses. The magistrates and other members of the body corporate then entered a protest against such illegal acts which in order to preserve their lives they had been forced to assent to.

On 6 August 1773 the *Ipswich Journal* wrote that the trial came before Lord Chief Justice De Grey at Bury Assizes. The trial was by an issue at the Court of the King's Bench. This was taken upon an information in the name of the Attorney General against several persons concerned in the riot upon the Moot Hall at Sudbury on 29 October 1771. At the trial Walden Hamner was acquitted and the other six persons were convicted of the said charge. They were to receive sentence in the Court of the King's Bench next Michaelmas term. Finally in February 1774, the paper reported that the persons found guilty of a riot in the Borough of Sudbury were brought to the King's Bench to receive sentence and were ordered by the court to suffer six months imprisonment. One inhabitant of the town was sentenced to pay one hundred pounds.

Thus in a few very short sentences the readers of the *Ipswich Journal* were told of the riot in Sudbury.[*]

By following these fascinating events as they made their tortuous way through the Court of the King's Bench one discovers a fascinating human story. This involved a

[*]   Ipswich Journals of the day

caring lawyer, a concerned member of the gentry, a surgeon and a group of Sudbury burgesses on the one side and a conniving ex Member of Parliament and some members of the Sudbury Corporation on the other.

So how was it, that what was in reality a very small and somewhat insignificant event in the eighteenth century was to become a cause célèbre in Suffolk? In part this was due to the people who were involved in the riot and also in the subsequent trial. However it was mainly due to the innate view that was slowly gaining ground that an Englishman however humble should never be bribed over the casting of his vote, which culminated in the Great Reform Bill of 1832 and such a man was John French.

In 1702 the House of Commons decreed that the son of a freeman or a man who had served an apprenticeship in Sudbury should be granted their freedom.* This not only entitled them to vote in elections but also allowed them to pasture their cow or horse on the town's common lands, which was of enormous importance to the poor of Sudbury and their families since it either meant that they could have somewhere to keep their animals, or if they did not have any such beasts they could get a grant in lieu.

Things came to a head in the spring of 1771 when the Sudbury Member of Parliament, one Walden Hamner, a Lincoln's Inn Barrister, was invited to the opening of the Common Lands. He decided to attend with his good friend Mr Blake as he had been hearing ugly rumours that the Corporation had ceased to formally grant the freedoms under stamp, as they were obliged to do to the qualifying burgesses. He had just been following a similar

* Journal of the House of Commons 2 November 1702/3

case, which was being tried in the Court of the King's Bench at the time. This was the case of William Smee, a barber, of Chelsea whose freedom had also been disallowed by the recently unseated Member of Parliament for Sudbury Thomas Fonnereau and several members of the Sudbury Corporation.

In the trial at the King's Bench after the 1771 riot, the most important man to be tried was Walden Hamner, a Lincoln's Inn Barrister. He believed wholeheartedly in the rights of the common man. He was supported in this view by a local landowner Henry Kedington and the Sudbury Surgeon John Deeks. The others who were put on trial were Mayhew French, who was John's younger brother, John Amy, John Berry, William Jones, Philip Stevens and Zorababel Ginn.

The Mayor, Alderman and the Capital Burgesses of the Borough of Sudbury met at the Moot Hall on 29 October 1771 when they issued an order that John Addison, John French and Richard French and thirty-seven others were to be admitted and inrolled as free burgesses as they were descended from Ancient Free Burgesses.

John French had a valid claim, which was based on the fact that his father Mayhew a cordwainer of Sudbury had been made a freeman. Mayhew had been bound and duly served as an apprentice to Thomas Dalton for an apprenticeship of seven years. His father John, a tailor of Sudbury, had paid for the indenture for this apprenticeship for him.

Amongst the others who were being invited to hold the office of the Freedom of the Borough were Isaac Frost, Philip Garwood, George Ginn, Thomas Hubbard the elder, Thomas Hubbard the younger, John Hubbard, John Jones the younger, Nathaniel Jones, Thomas Jones and Henry Jones.

Peter Delande, Thomas Fonnereau's agent, had approached all these men, as he wanted to find out which way they were proposing to vote in the next election. They had independently decided not to vote for his man Thomas Fonnereau. When the Mayor and Corporation met in the Moot Hall on 18 October 1771, Delande instigated a complaint saying the claims of the new freemen were variously unjust. The Court therefore decided that these newly appointed freemen should appear at a Court of Orders and Decrees on Tuesday 29 October 1771* at 10 o'clock in order that they could substantiate their claims and if proven they would then legally be entitled to be admitted.

On 29 October, the Court duly met and after the enunciation of the ancient customs by which the Borough of Sudbury would give the Title of Freemen, the proceedings were begun. The Court decreed that every person who was duly qualified according to the ancient customs would be entitled to be admitted and sworn into the office of Freeman. Peter Delande immediately raised his objections and the men were disallowed from becoming freemen, which caused total disbelief amongst them. Walden Hamner immediately took up their case and argued it very strongly in an impassioned speech. He firmly believed that if the men lost their right to become freemen they would not only lose their rights of franchise but also they would lose their rights of pasturage which was a great consideration for a poor man. Alderman Henry Kedington ably supported him, as he had been involved in Sudbury Borough politics for some time.

Many of the men from the town attended the meeting to support John Addison and John and Richard French

*   Court of Orders and Decrees 29 November 1771

in their claim.

After a couple of hours, William Strutt, a Capital Burgess, made a motion which was immediately passed to set up a secret committee to enquire into the rights of the claimants. However the bystanders fiercely opposed this motion and a long and sometimes noisy debate followed which carried on for a further nine hours. The noise level gradually increased and a small piece of cornice fell down. The Mayor and Corporation were then prevented from leaving the Moot Hall and as night fell, they were forced to sit in darkness as the townspeople jeered as they ate their suppers and lit their own candles. In this darkened atmosphere, a large chain was rattled and many of the men made roaring noises. Even though the Mayor's party was unable to go to their dinner this did not prevent Walden Hamner from departing to the local inn for his meal. By the time he returned to the darkened and noisy Moot Hall, the Mayor and Aldermen had agreed to the three men, John Addison and John and Richard French, being admitted to the Office of Ancient Free Burgess to prevent any further trouble. At this point, someone got a message out of the room and the Dragoons from Colchester Garrison were summoned to come and relieve the situation and dispel the riot.

On 27 January 1772 an Information was exhibited against Walden Hamner and the Sudbury Eight who were deemed to be the main perpetrators of the riot and instrumental in its start. They were Henry Kedington, Gentleman and Alderman of the Borough of Sudbury, John Deeks, surgeon, John Berry, weaver, John Amy, tanner, Philip Stevens, weaver, Mayhew French the younger, labourer, Zorababel Ginn, blacksmith and William Jones, shoemaker. All pleaded not guilty to the charges made against them.

At a Court of the Borough of Sudbury on 29 January 1772, a protest to the consent and agreement of the admission of John Addison and John and Richard French was made. There then followed a detailed description of the riot from the perspective of the Aldermen and the Capital Burgesses who stated as recorded in the Court Book.* 'Whereby a wicked, seditious and turbulent multitude of ill advised men under the false pretence of asserting their title to the Freedom of Sudbury disturbed the peace and good government of the Borough. The Mayor and Aldermen had been prevented from returning home, and by violent means had been imprisoned in the Moot Hall until nine at night, thus depriving them of any sustenance. Also they alleged inhuman outrages and horrid imprecations were perpetrated in the dark as well as describing their terror as stones, pieces of timber and buckets were thrown at them which threatened them.' This was further amplified in the Affidavits for the Prosecution** sworn by Herbert Russell, weaver, William Humphrey Junior, brazier, Samuel Outing, brazier, James Sillito, whitesmith and Robert Feakes, tinner.

Herbert Russell said that at half past ten on the 29 October 1771, he was standing at the door of the Black Boy Inn when he saw the gentlemen of the Corporation being obstructed from entering the Moot Hall by a very large crowd. He then saw the Member for Sudbury Mr Walden Hamner coming down the street followed by another great crowd. Mr Hamner then said something to the gathering, which Russell could not hear as he was too far away. However as a result of what Hamner had said the crowd followed him into the Moot Hall and pushed

*   Sudbury Court of Orders and Decrees
**   Affidavits KB/18 at the Public Record Office

aside the Constable. Between eleven and twelve o'clock
Russell walked to the Hall as he was one of the persons
who had been summoned to appear and verify their claims
to the Freedom of Sudbury at a Court of Orders and
Decrees. When he reached the hall he found several hundred people there who were behaving in a very disorderly
manner by shouting and abusing the Mayor. He then
heard Mr Hamner speak, which caused the shouting to
increase, and then Mayhew French the Younger struck
him and several others had stamped on him and kicked
him. He was therefore forced to leave the Court and added
that the injuries, which he sustained, had prevented him
from working for several days.

William Humphrey enlarged on Russell's testimony by
stating that he heard Mr Hamner's words which were
'You shall all go up, all go up'. He continued by saying
he went into the Hall later in the afternoon and tried to
speak to his father who was sitting on the Bench but he
was held and dragged out of the Court and his coat was
torn. He concluded his deposition by saying that the
people were becoming increasingly violent and were
shouting out that they would keep the Corporation in
the Hall. Samuel Outing's deposition was that while
Walden Hamner was speaking he waved his hand which
he felt was meant to further encourage the riotous crowd
in their unruly behaviour. James Sillitoe said that Mr
Hamner said that he would stand by them even if he had
to stay a month. He further added that Mayhew French
the Younger had declared that none of the Gentlemen,
by which he meant the Corporation, should leave until
they all had their freedoms. He also said that French and
Philip Stevens stood at the door of the Hall and would
not let him leave. Finally Robert Feakes stated that he
had heard Mr Hamner say as he was coming down the

stairs that he was glad that he had come to serve them and he then doffed his hat to them.

The first affidavit for the defence was sworn under oath by John Berry and John Amy, weavers, Zorababel Ginn, blacksmith, Mayhew French, labourer, and William Jones, cordwainer from the Borough of Sudbury.* Each of the men spoke for themselves and said that they had all reached the age of twenty-one years. They had also served an apprenticeship of seven years, which entitled them to become a freeman of the Borough. Further they had all wished to exercise the same Rights of Freedom that their fathers and their masters as free burgesses had done. These rights not only allowed them to vote for their Member of Parliament for Sudbury but also and much more importantly it allowed for the enjoyment of the profits and the benefits of the Common lands, which had been granted to all free burgesses of Sudbury. All the deponents said that these rights had only been disputed and called into question very recently. The Mayor, Aldermen and the Capital Burgesses had caused great dissension amongst the people of Sudbury when they disallowed the freedom of such of the poor free burgesses who had neither been entered nor inrolled on stamps. They also said that it was the will of the Mayor and Corporation that these deponents and other poor freemen should all be deprived of their freedom of the Borough. Further these deponents had only just learned of the House of Commons resolution of 1702 which gave the terms under which they could be admitted to the freedom. However they realized that the current policy of the Sudbury Corporation was only to inroll freemen who had purchased their freedom, which was a comparatively new

* KB/18

method. This denial of their rights had been instigated by Thomas Fonnereau Esq formerly the Member of Parliament for Sudbury, who had advised the Mayor and his Corporation in these matters.

The deponents said they were very alarmed at this new departure and said that if they had known about the new rules they would have complied with them. They also said that the Mayor had constantly put off giving the burgesses their freedoms on the pretext that they had to wait for a Court of Appeals and Decrees. When such a Court was convened however they were then told that there was too much business to be dealt with so no freedoms were granted, thus disenfranchising a number of men who should have been made free burgesses. They concluded that this was to the electoral advantage of Thomas Fonnereau and they all felt they were at a further disadvantage in this as they could not vote and they had also lost their rights of pasturage of the Common lands. This not only affected the widows and families of the freemen but also themselves.

All the deponents said that when they heard that a Court was going to be summoned for the inrollment of free burgesses on 29 October, they decided to attend in order to establish their rights to be admitted and inrolled in due form. They went to the Moot Hall but like many of their fellows they did not attempt to enter as the Mayor and the Corporation were transacting their business. Further they did not attempt in any way to interrupt the business of the Court until the Mayor ordered that the Court be dissolved. As things had changed radically they decided to interrupt the proceedings to make an objection to the formation of the Committee to look into their rights.

They said that some time after this, Mr Walden Hamner arrived at the Hall and passed through them. When they

saw him they all gave a loud shout for joy since they felt
he would prevent any injury or injustice being done to
the poor free burgesses. Also they felt that they were more
likely to obtain their admission to the freedom through
his intervention. All these deponents said that on account
of their poverty and lack of friends in the Corporation,
they thought of him as their saviour and they had no
other way of showing their thankfulness except by shouting. However Mr Hamner told them to be quiet and to
act peacefully. He then made a speech stating that he had
come to the Court to assist and support the free burgesses
over their rights to their freedoms. In reply William Strutt
the younger proposed that a committee should be set up
to look into the claims of those who were asking for their
admissions to the freedom and to decide who had a claim
and who did not. This resulted in all the poor freemen
shouting out 'No Committee,' as this idea gave them great
offence. Mr Walden Hamner replied that instead of a
Committee, the claims should be judged by this Court as
many of the poor freemen had dockets of their father's
freedom or other awards to the same effect.

After this speech, the Corporation went back in to the
Hall and the Town Clerk began to examine the claims of
Mr John Addison by looking in the Court Books. During
this time, there was silence in the Court. John Addison
asked whether he could produce a witness of his birth and
evidence of his father's freedom as he felt this would save
the Court time. However the Court would not consent to
this, whereupon another dispute broke out, this time
between some of the Capital Burgesses. The Mayor, Mr
Oliver, then again ordered that the Court be dissolved which
caused another great uproar and more confusion.

All the deponents said that since the last general election
this kind of dissolution had occurred every time the poor

freemen had applied for their admission, but they had not insulted John Oliver, William Humphrey or Peter Delande. However they did say that they and many others went into that part of the Moot Hall called the Court and argued with the Mayor and the Aldermen about the hardship caused by taking away their freedom. They added that many of them had a better right to their freedom than those who were part of the Corporation since many of them had procured their freedom at a private inrolment by purchase, a process which was previously unknown to the poor freemen.

The deponents continued that the Hall was now full of many men who were very exasperated by the proceedings. They all agreed that they shouted at the Mayor and Aldermen saying that they would not allow them to have any food or drink until they had admitted and inrolled such of the free burgesses who had the right to their freedoms. In this, they were supported by some of the Capital Burgesses.

Mr William Jones stated that he went and spoke with Mr Peter Delande in a very civil manner about the general hardships caused by taking away their rights to the freedom. He also pointed out that the unhappy differences in the town were in great measure caused by him under the direction of Mr Fonnereau. Mr Delande then asked whether he would vote for the said Mr Fonnereau. Jones knew that he, as a good freeman, had the right to vote as he pleased and told Delande so. He said that Mr Delande did not answer him so he reiterated his question again and again. He added that when they had been at Bury St Edmunds, he had been told he could receive his freedom if he voted for Mr Fonnereau. When he refused, this had caused Mr Delande to conceive a great dislike and prejudice against him.

All the deponents said that a few of their number did get on the tables but not until the Court was dissolved. They also said that some of them insulted Mr Delande by calling him Mounsee meaning Monsieur as he was of French extraction. They all felt that the confusion was in the main due both to Mr Delande and Mr Fonnereau who both wanted to deprive the poor of their birthrights. They then added that they asked both Mr Oliver and Mr Humphrey how they would feel if their children were similarly treated. Finally they said that the latter had only recently become a Christian and therefore he should act on Christian principles.

The deponents all agreed that they saw some boys getting up on the beams at this stage of the proceedings to climb across the Hall, and this had inadvertently brought down some of the mouldings, which were only one quarter of an inch thick. However they were adamant that this was not done deliberately, but was because of the large numbers of men in the Hall had made it so hot that some windows were broken to let in some air by the men on the outside. They added that some of the stones had even been thrown by William Humphrey's son and also the son of Mr Carter, an Alderman. All the deponents denied any of these charges of breaking the windows or any other outrage.

Deponent Philip Stevens said that he did stand at the door of the Hall to hear the debate but did not do any wrong.

Mayhew French denied that he had struck Herbert Russell, as the latter had sworn in his affidavit.

After the swearing of the affidavits the course of the legal proceedings began.

On June 1772 a plea was entered on the rolls of the Court of the King's Bench* between the King as represented

* Court of the King's Bench Rolls KB29 431

by James Burrows Esquire, and Walden Hamner and the rest of the defendants. They were impeached of certain trespasses, contempts and misdemeanours. The sheriff of the County of Suffolk was then ordered to bring the defendants to the Court on the Morrow of Holy Trinity to answer to this plea. This same day was given to James Burrows. On the Friday after the Morrow of Holy Trinity, all the defendants duly attended the Court. Walden Hamner represented himself, as did Henry Kedington. The other men were represented by John Wace whom they had instructed to be their Attorney. They heard the Information, which had been laid against them and all pleaded not guilty. They then placed themselves upon the Country, as did James Burrows.*

The trial was set to take place on the Morrow of All Souls. In the rolls, a Verdict Judgement was again signed upon a Parchment Stamp to the form of the Statute for the case to be heard between our Lord the King in Westminster and Walden Hamner and the other seven defendants. They were to be tried upon their oath in order to discover whether they were guilty of the premise of contempt and misdemeanour of which they were impeached. James Burrows and John Wace were in attendance.

On 20 November 1772, being the Morrow of All Souls, the Sheriff was ordered by William, Lord Mansfield at Westminster on behalf of the King to bring all the defendants from their prison in his Bailiwick to trial. Again in the rolls the defendants were arraigned for trespass, contempt riots and unlawful assemblies as well as assault and misdemeanours.

However the Sheriff had not returned the writ to Wace, thus negating the proceedings. As a result the Court was

* KB 29/431

adjourned until the Octave of Saint Hilary and all the defendants were taken into prison, with the exception of Walden Hamner, to await their trial by jury.

Before the trial could take place at the Octave of Saint Hilary 1773, the rolls of the King's Bench showed an entry on 12 November 1772 that Zorababel Ginn the blacksmith late of Sudbury had made a confession against the Information for a trespass, contempt, riot and unlawful assembly of which he was impeached. Ginn pleaded guilty to the charges.* On 5 February 1773, being in the Octave of Saint Hilary, both James Burrows Esquire and Walden Hamner, John Wace and the other defendants came to the Court. Once again the Sheriff had not returned the writ to John Wace nor had he performed any of his duties in the respect of the trial. Therefore it was decreed that a jury none of whom should be related to the defendants should come before the Judge as the representative of the King fifteen days after Easter and the case was again adjourned. By this time the Prosecutor James Burrows had become Sir James Burrows. He and Walden Hamner and the other defendants together with their attorney again came to the Court where they found that yet again the Sheriff had not returned the writ. So once again the trial was adjourned and it was decreed that the Court would sit and the trial by jury should take place on the Morrow of Holy Trinity.

The Rolls of the Court of the King's Bench again entered a plea between our Lord the King and Walden Hamner, Esquire, Henry Kedington, Gentleman, John Deeks, John Berry, John Amy, Philip Stevens, Mayhew French and William Jones. Also the Verdict Judgement was again

---

*   Roll 14 number 8 of the Roll of Trinity Term of the twelfth Year of George the Third signed upon Parchment Stamp to the form of the Statute in the case to be held between the King and all the defendants.*

Henry Kedington died in 1773 and the trial eventually began when the Sheriff of Suffolk was commanded to bring the defendants before the Justices on Thursday 29 July 1773 to the Assizes at Bury Saint Edmunds. These Justices were the Honourable Sir William de Grey, Knight and Chief Justice of his Majesty's Court of Common Pleas, and Sir Richard Aston, one of the Justices assigned by the King to hold pleas. Three of the jurors who had been called were sworn in and they were Christopher Metcalfe Esquire of Hawstead, John Sparke Esquire, and Ezekiah Sparke Esquire both of Walsham le Willows. The other nominated jurors had not appeared so the Sheriff at the request of Edward Thurlow Esquire Attorney General chose the rest of the jury from the bystanders who were attending the Court. The names of the jurors were written as the law decreed. They were Richard and John Clarke, Philip Whincrop, Thomas Denny, Thomas Langley, Robert Lawter, William Sparke, John Woodward and Bigsby Buck. They were all sworn in as jurors in the proper fashion.

The Session of the Court then began with the public proclamation being made for our Lord the King about who should inform the Judges as to outcome of the deliberations of the jury of the case in hand. One of the Sergeants at Law, William Whittaker Esquire, stepped forward and offered to do this. The Court then began to take the Inquest by the jurors. At this point all the defendants took the oath to speak the truth concerning

---

*   Roll 8 of the Michaelmas Term in the fourteenth year of the reign of George the Third KB 29/431 and 433

the matters of the Information against them.

After the jurors had heard the evidence and made their deliberations they took the oath and declared that Walden Hamner who had defended himself was not guilty of the Premises in the Information. However they said on oath that John Deeks, John Berry, John Amy, Philip Stevens, Mayhew French and William Jones who had pleaded for themselves with the aid of their attorney were guilty of the Premises in the third count alleged against them although they were not guilty of the Premises in the first, second fourth and fifth counts. They were in fact found not guilty of the offences of trespass, contempt, unlawful assembly, assault or misdemeanour but only of the grave offence of riot. Thus Walden Hamner could leave the Court without any stain on his character, and in May 1774 he was created a Baronet. However the other defendants including Mayhew were to be taken back into custody. All the defendants were held in the Gaol at Bury St Edmunds until the final judgement was made. This took place on the Morrow of the Purification of the Blessed Virgin Mary being 5 February 1774. John Deeks was given a sentence of a hundred pound fine and the others were sentenced to six months in gaol.

Life then got back to normal for the French family who had stood up so forcibly for their rights and John was in fact made a Freeman of Sudbury on 9 July 1778.

His two eldest daughters Mary and Alice did not get married. Mary died in 1782 in the town and Alice was still living in her own house in Sudbury in 1798. The owner was Joseph Hayward. He also rented a house to Alice's sister Sarah who had been baptized on 6 March 1766. She also never married.

John and Mary's fourth child James was born in 1762 and he died at the age of five in 1772, as did his brother

Thomas who was born and died that year. Anthony was baptized on 14 November 1769 and the couple's youngest child George on 27 November 1777.

George did not follow his father as a Weaver but pursued various careers. He married Margaret Woolnough in the early years of the nineteenth century but she died on 4 March 1803 and is buried at Saint Mary's Church Bury Saint Edmunds. The couple had the one son George Anthony and it is most likely that Margaret died in childbirth. She was only twenty-three.

After the death of his wife, George who had been working for his Uncle Samuel in the George Inn moved away from Suffolk together with his young son to escape his sad memories.

In 1805 George became the Licensee of an Inn in Castle Hedingham across the border in Essex.* This was in all probability the King's Head. On 7 August 1805, he applied as a publican for a marriage licence to marry Ann Tomlinson the daughter of the town solicitor. The couple lived happily in Castle Hedingham until 1813 and during this time they had their first daughter, Frances.

In early 1814 George and Ann decided that his future was better served with his nephew John French who was by this time the Proprietor of French and Woods the Coaching firm of Chelmsford. They had met up at all the family weddings in the first years of the nineteenth century and John had most probably asked his uncle to join him in the firm.

As a result of their deliberations, George moved with Ann and Frances to Maldon in Essex where he established his own business as an adjunct to French and Woods.

* Register of the persons licensed to a Particular Inn in Castle Hedingham

This ran the coaches and waggons between the East Coast and Chelmsford and from thence to London. His van also left his office for the capital each Friday at twelve o'clock.

Ann looked after George Anthony as well as her daughter Frances and on 8 August, she had her second daughter Ann in Maldon. She had another, Eliza, who died as a child. The business flourished and George and his nephew John's family continued to be very friendly as they got on so well. George was one of the witnesses at John Junior's marriage to Sarah Dixon.

George Anthony learned his trade as a Coachmaster from his father and cousin and later moved down to London in the early eighteen thirties. On 25 February 1834 he married Emily Inskipp at Saint Clements Church Hastings and they had one daughter, Elizabeth.

George and Ann continued to prosper and they both died very close together with George dying on 18 August 1841 and Ann on 27 September 1842. Ann ran the company with the help of John Gainsford until her death. This is shown by the advertisement that Ann put in the *Chelmsford Chronicle* in October 1841 inviting all the Company's creditors and debtors to contact her within the month.*

George in his Will left the business and his home at Hill House to his wife and thereafter to his son. He left George Anthony and his two daughters a third share each of his share capital.

Ann and Frances continued to live in the town of Maldon together very happily until Ann married Charles Wright the local schoolmaster at the National School in the town. They had one daughter, Emma.

*   Chelmsford Chronicle 8 October 1841

Meanwhile George Anthony moved to Birmingham from Mile End Old Town in London where his daughter Elizabeth had been was born. He continued to work as a Coach Proprietor and to build on his inheritance from his father. Elizabeth married Charles Rowe while the family was living in Birmingham.

John French himself died on 22 November 1780 aged forty-nine. His widow Mary died fifteen years later on 13 March 1795. The couple were both buried at Saint Peter's Church Sudbury.

CHAPTER 9

Mayhew French
1704–1771

Mayhew French was the second son of John French and his wife Martha. John and Martha Mayhew had been married at Saint Peter's Church in Sudbury where John was a tailor. Their first son John was also baptized at Saint Peter's on 28 September 1701 and Mayhew on 12 December 1704.

They had another son, Anthony, whose baptism I have failed so far to find, but he died on 29 November 1710.

It is likely that the family moved over Ballingdon Bridge as they began worshipping at All Saints Church in that part of the town during the years around 1710, as the burial records when Anthony was buried at Saint Gregory's Church stated that his parents were of the Parish of All Saints. Mayhew had four probably five other siblings. Elizabeth was baptized on 17 August 1710. Robert on 6 March 1715, Catherine on 11 March 1717 and Sarah on 11 July 1721. There is a possibility that there was another daughter Martha also born in this period.

On 30 April 1724, Mayhew was apprenticed to Thomas Dalton of Sudbury who was a cordwainer.* A cordwainer was a tradesman who worked with leather. This embraced a number of jobs varying from small ones like the making

* Apprenticeship List 30 April 1724 at the Public Record Office

of bottles and shoes to much larger tasks such as the making of horse harnesses.

His father John, who was a tailor of Sudbury, paid ten shillings a year for his indenture for the apprenticeship. This training lasted for seven years.

In 1726, Mayhew married Mary Rose of Little Waldingfield. She was the daughter of Richard and Elizabeth and the couple had their first son Mayhew in Little Waldingfield.

They then moved back to Sudbury where the rest of their children were baptized.

In 1761, Mayhew applied to be admitted as one of the free burgesses of Sudbury. He stated that he had served his full seven-year term as an apprentice by Indenture to Thomas Dalton, a cordwainer of the town and thus fulfilled the requirement to be admitted. At a Court of Orders and Decrees, he was duly admitted as a free burgess.* After this Mayhew started to take an active part in the corporate life in Sudbury. He had already been appointed by the Parish of Saint Peter's to be an Overseer of the Trades in the town in 1733 thus following the example of his maternal grandfather Robert Mayhew. Robert was the Parish butcher and a freeman of Sudbury, who had been a Surveyor of the Fishmarket amongst his other such duties.**

Mayhew and Mary's first-born child Mayhew was baptized on 10 September 1728 but he died as a child at the age of eleven. The next child to be born, his brother Anthony, was now the eldest of the boys. He was baptized at Saint Peter's Church in Sudbury on 9 December 1730. He did not follow in his father's footsteps and become a

---

*   Court of Orders and Decrees EE501/2/10 Bury Record Office
** Court of Orders and Decrees EE501/2/9

cordwainer but instead became a baker and was very successful in this work. On 15 April 1754, he married Alice Stearns of the Parish of Saint Peter's. His brother John supported him at the wedding.

During the next ten years Anthony established himself both commercially and socially as a member of the middle classes. He became a sidesman at Saint Peter's Church and also attended the Annual Vestry meeting each year to vote for the Church Warden which was a most coveted lay office in the running of the Church.

He also realized that a further route to social preferment was to become a freeman of the borough of Sudbury. After researching the Ancient Laws on this topic, he persuaded his father to apply for this privilege as he had served his apprenticeship in the town under Thomas Dalton. Mayhew became a Freeman on 9 January 1761 and Anthony followed him on 3 April of the same year.* However he did not just become a Free Burgess as he paid the requisite sum of eight pounds and eight shillings and the customary two buckets for the privilege of also being admitted to the Freedom of the Common Lands.** This not only showed his social status but also that he was doing very well financially.

This is further demonstrated by the fact that he also was diversifying his business interests. In 1767 he placed an advertisement stating that he was responsible for the letting of his Inn known as the George which was at the time occupied by his brother Samuel.***

Anthony and Alice had a son Anthony who was baptized on 26 June 1761. They had also had another

*   Court of Orders and Decrees 9 January 1761
** Court of Orders and Decrees 4 April 1761
*** Ipswich Journal 26 January 1767

son James who was baptized on 11 April 1755. There was in all probability an elder son Anthony who died, as did his son Joseph who died aged three on 19 December 1780.

One of Anthony's last public duties before his untimely death was to vote for the new Mayor of Sudbury, as the current incumbent John Oliver his was going to live in Melford with his family. Anthony appeared as one of the forty-eight free tenants of the Borough.*

Anthony died on 26 July 1780 at the age of forty-nine. His son Anthony took over the baker's shop and continued to run it successfully. He also followed in his father's footsteps and became a Freeman of Sudbury on 18 June 1782. His mother vouched for the fact that her husband who had purchased his freedom of the Commons by a docket under the hands of the then Mayor, now deceased, and that Anthony was their son.**

Anthony continued to carry on his father's civic duties and in August 1782, he subscribed to the building of Ship of War for the service of the Public.*** He donated a guinea, which was by no means a small sum. Also on 12 July 1787, he served on the jury to hear a case of riot which was an ironical fact considering his family's part in the 1781 Riot.****

On 2 March 1786, he went before the Church Authorities to purchase a Licence for a hundred pounds to marry Sarah Ginn who was his cousin, John French's wife Ann's sister. She was born in 1759 in Sudbury although she was living in Dedham at the time of their

---

*   Assembly of Aldermen and Free Burgesses 25 November 1777
**   Inrolled in cocket Book 165
***   List of Subscribers
**** Jury at the Quarter Sessions 12 July 1787

marriage. John, later of Chelmsford, accompanied him
to the hearing. Anthony stated he was a baker and John
a victualler with both being of the Parish of Saint Peter's
of Sudbury. The couple lived in Sudbury where Anthony
worked and they had the one son Anthony who was born
on 16 April 1788. This child was born after the death of
his father, which occurred on 3 October 1787, and he too
soon died.

Mayhew's next son Samuel was baptized on 9 July 1735
again at Saint Peter's Church. Not a great deal of information could be found about Samuel although like
Anthony he was a baker by trade and was also in business
in the grocery trade in Sudbury. He also lived at the
George Inn in 1767. It appears that he and Anthony were
very close as brothers as well as doing a great deal of
business together. He was made a freeman of the Borough
on 9 July 1778 and became very interested in politics. So
much so that during one of Sir John Cox Hippesley's
campaigns to become the Member of Parliament for Sudbury, he together with Anthony accompanied Cox
Hippersley not only around the town but also to the hust-
ings. He also like his brother Anthony was an active
member of the Church and attended the Annual Vestry
meeting on 20 April 1775.

He married Hannah but so far no trace of this marriage
has been found. His son Samuel was born about 1771
and his daughter Hannah was baptized at Saint Gregory's
Church on 23 March 1780. Six further children were born
to the couple. Samuel died on 20 September 1793.

His son, Samuel followed in his father's footsteps by
becoming a baker and he also applied for and was granted
the Freedom of the Borough in 1802. Sometime after that
Samuel moved to 46 Mount Street in Grosvenor Square
London and worked as grocer. Meanwhile in Sudbury,

Samuel's mother had fallen on hard times and by 1809 her son was finding it well nigh impossible to help her financially. He had helped with the financial drain caused by his father's long illness, but the ongoing help required for his mother and his seven brothers and sisters who were still living at home was beyond him financially. As a result of these problems he wrote to Sir John for his help in these matters.*

Maybe as result of this letter or when he had sufficient means, Samuel later returned to Sudbury to live with his sister Hannah. By 1823, he was a Church Warden at Saint Peter's Church, an office he held for many years and in 1828 he was voting in the Parliamentary Poll of that year as a baker.

Over the following years Samuel became increasingly more comfortably off and thus became a true member of the rising Middle Classes.

He lived in a house with three rods and fourteen poles of land. He also owned a further acre and one rod and one pole of land, which on the 1841 Tithe map is described as a Market Garden.** This land is where Vanners Silk Factory now stands. He also had four other properties one of which was a double fronted messuage and another one was a single fronted messuage. These were rented to James Barrow, James Byford and Widow Wire as well as to his late brother James.

In the Census of 1841, he is listed as being of independent means and was living in Sepulchre Street. He died on 5 June 1848 and is buried in the graveyard at Saint Gregory's Church, where the grave still stands His

* Letter from Samuel French to Sir John Hippesley in the Suffolk Record Office
** Tithe Map of Sudbury 1841

sister continued to live in his house under the terms of Samuel's Will when he left his land and messuages to his nephew Josiah Jones,* on the condition that his Aunt lived in the house for the rest of her natural life. She was still there in 1851 in the Census of that year.

Mayhew and Mary's next son Mayhew the younger was baptized on 8 September 1742 at Saint Peter's Church. He worked as a labourer in the town after his apprenticeship. On 21 October 1766 at Acton Church he married Jane Clark who lived at Acton. His brother James who acted as a Witness supported him at the wedding. Jane was the daughter of Philip Shelley's mother's second husband and the Shelleys and the French family both lived at Wiggen End on the western outskirts of Sudbury. Mayhew and Jane had three children Jane born in 1767, Mayhew in 1772 and John who only lived for two months in 1774.

Mayhew must have been of a somewhat fiery nature as was shown by the part he took in the 1771 riot. Also, over the years, there were a series of disputes amongst the families who lived in this somewhat complex community of Wiggen End with Mayhew taking an active part. One of these disputes was settled at the General Quarter Sessions of the Borough of Sudbury before the Mayor Thomas Hawes Esquire and Stephen Oliver, one of the Justices of the King. At the court, Jane Mayhew's wife accused Philip Shelley of hitting her in such a manner that she thought he was going to kill her.** The judgement of the Court was given in Jane's favour and Shelley and his two supporters had to pay 40 shillings and 20 shillings respectively as recognizance of the fact that Philip and

*   Will of Samuel French 1848
** Quarter Sessions 16 October 1783

his family and friends should keep the peace especially towards Jane French. However if they kept the peace this recognizance would be made void.

In 1783 and very soon after the Court case, Mayhew entered into a 'Rights Close' agreement between himself Philip Shelley blacksmith, Thomas Smith, blacksmith, William Bush, husbandman, and Thomas Clarke of Acton also a husbandman. This was over the recent conversion of the tenements in Wiggen Close into four cottages in which they were then living. It also stated that these men would have a share in the pump, paths and passages.

Their disputes seemed well and truly over by this time and in 1784 Mayhew attended the marriage of Samuel Shelley and acted as a witness.

On 10 July 1778 Mayhew became a Freeman of the Borough* by birth as being the son of Mayhew despite his being found guilty of riot in 1774, and he died on 19 September 1784 at the age of forty-two.

Mayhew and Mary's fifth son James was baptized on 3 June 1745. Very little is known about James who was a Private on the Middlesex Militia. He, like his four brothers, was made a freeman of Sudbury in May 1780. The next event in his life was that he married Sarah Betts on 27 September 1781 and his brother John and their mutual friend Elias Cleare a laceman of the town witnessed the marriage. Afterwards, James returned to live and work in Sudbury where his brother Samuel the baker gave him a job. James and Sarah had two children in Sudbury. Their eldest child was James who was born on 26 October 1781. They then had a little girl Sarah on 12 June 1785 but poor Sarah died in childbirth. This

*   Court of Orders and Decrees 9 July 1778

appears to have devastated James and he suffered greatly from this loss. The result of this was that he was not able to work or pay his rent.

In April 1790, he was rejected for the Poll of that year on account of the fact that his rent had been paid by the Workhouse Corporation. He was still styled as a baker.*

Later James lived in one of his nephew Samuel's houses until he himself died on 20 November 1804.

There is also very little known about Mayhew and Mary's youngest child Mary who was baptized on 2 February 1747. When Mary was twenty years of age she got married by licence as she was under age. At the licencing hearing her bridegroom-to-be stated Mayhew French was her natural father. By this time her mother Mary had died and was buried on 1 July 1761. The young couple were married at Saint Peter's Church Sudbury on 11 January 1768. After the marriage they went to live in Bocking in Essex where James Collins her new husband was a postilion.

Mayhew Senior continued to live in the town until his own death ten years later in November 1771 a month after the riot in which his sons John and Mayhew were involved. One wonders whether this caused him so much distress that it caused his demise.

---

*   Transcript of the Poll Book of the Parliamentary Election of 18 June 1790 published by Allan Berry

CHAPTER 10

John French
1670–1748

After 1688, England experienced a period of peace and prosperity. There was very little in the way of political disturbance and even the Jacobites failed to cause a great deal of waves. England was mainly a country of small villages and hamlets interspersed with little towns, which were mostly built around the coastline and had been developed for trade. Her population was still very small, being under five million. However life was very slowly changing forever. The main causes of change were the combined influences of the Industrial Revolution and the Agricultural Revolution together with the rise of Methodism and the gradual increase in the membership of the Church of England. These all exerted a tremendous influence on people's lives. However the towns were still small and by today's standard were little more than villages.

In East Anglia where this story begins the population was declining with the reduction both in the wool trade and in the number of agricultural labourers. The latter group had been greatly affected by the rising number of enclosures and the new farming practices. The main result of this was that many families made their way to London and other big cities and towns.

However life in the small towns was pretty grim, with overcrowding being a problem combined as it was with a lack of sanitation. The rich did have cesspits but for the ordinary person there was only the road to use, thus making them in fact open sewers. These roads were also unpaved and filthy. The main consequence of all this was that diseases such as typhoid, dysentery and smallpox stalked the towns and cities and attacked rich or poor alike. Thus very few children survived infancy and childhood and even adults faced a hard life. Many of both the young and the old also took to drink to escape life's miseries and this in its turn killed numerous people.

Law and order was also minimal with a limited number of Parish Constables, so crime was rife. Finally famine was often a problem as well in 1709,1713, 1727 and 1740.

The Middle Classes at this time mostly supported the Whig party. However this support did not extend to the Prime Minister Robert Walpole, as his was a conservative political creed based on all the old traditions. The Whigs had quickly acquired money from the new industries born of the Industrial Revolution and they put this money into property. However despite their change in fortune they did not change either culturally or philosophically

In the towns like Sudbury local government was in the control of the Borough Council whose members were predominantly small businessmen, merchants and lawyers. This group of people were doing very well and taking advantage of not only the good terms of trade affecting the country but also of all the new industrial developments.

Life for the artisans however remained as hard as ever since they were working fourteen-hour days for very low wages. If they were lucky they kept their jobs as their employers combined with others to survive. However life was not all bad, as there was plenty of cheap food available in the county towns.

This was however a period of great stability of life and to be a vigorous and resourceful man was a great benefit. The opportunities for such a man were enormous if he took advantage of the good trading conditions and all the new working processes. A man could not only become financially secure but also could rise socially up the scale. There were many of these men among the East Anglian French Family during the next three hundred years.

John French was a reasonably comfortable tailor who lived in Sudbury. He married Martha Mayhew on 19 June 1701 at Saint Peter's Church in the town. Martha was the daughter of Robert Mayhew and his wife Martha the former Martha Mills who had been married at Saint Peter's Church on 15 March 1680. Robert was the son of Robert Mayhew who was a Freeman of the Borough of Sudbury. He was a butcher who had been born in Great Waldingfield and had later moved to Sudbury. His son continued in the butchery trade and also was a freeman. He had been a Surveyor of the Fish Market in 1726 some seven years before his grandson Mayhew was an Overseer of Trades.* Both men took their civic duties very seriously.

John and Martha had a very large family. Their eldest son John was baptized at Saint Peter's Church where they had been married on 28 September 1702 and it was recorded that alms were given to the Church. Mayhew followed him on 12 November 1704. He was baptised at Saint Gregory's Church. A third child Anthony was born some time between 1704 and 1710 when he died and was buried at Saint Gregory's Church on 29 November, although he was from the Parish of All Saints.

During this time it is likely that the family moved over

*   Cocket Book 1726

Ballingdon Bridge and it was therefore in the Parish of All Saints where the rest of the families were baptised. Their first daughter was Elizabeth who was baptized on 17 August 1712 and who died on 3 October in the same year. The couple had another daughter the next year who they also christened Elizabeth on 24 October 1713. She was followed by Robert on 6 March 1715, Catherine on 20 March 1717 and Sarah on 11 July 1721. It is very likely that they had a daughter Martha who was married to Samuel Edgar on 6 July 1735.

Martha died on 6 January 1756 as a Widow and John most probably in 1748. He had been financially successful as he had paid for his son Mayhew's indenture.

Thus it can be seen from this study that the French Family of East Anglia showed all the main attributes which we normally associate with that most English of phenomenon, the 'Rise of the Middle Classes'.

They most certainly used their natural intelligence and drive combined with their organizational abilities and technical expertise to slowly rise through that social space which existed between the working and middle classes. Moreover many of their number ran their own businesses and others entered the professions.

They were also as a family very much influenced by the new political and religious mores of the times in which they lived and incorporated these into their own philosophies of life.

However and, most importantly of all, they were a very family oriented group of men and women. In the bad times they helped each other and throughout the three hundred years of this study they remained, for the most part, constant and good friends with each other. So all in all the French family could be said to be the very essence of the Rising Middle Classes.

Index